T0147360

Three <u>Strikes</u> and You Are Not <u>Out</u>

A True Story

by Ms. Paulajean Anne Anderson

authorHOUSE®

AuthorHouse™
1663 Liberty Drive
Bloomington, IN 47403
www.authorhouse.com
Phone: 1-800-839-8640

The names mentioned in this book have been changed so that
there will be no hard feelings. Similarities to actual events may be
incidental even though some of the stories discussed are true.

First published by AuthorHouse 3/7/2011

ISBN: 978-1-4567-3923-2 (sc)
ISBN: 978-1-4567-3922-5 (dj)
ISBN: 978-1-4567-3921-8 (e)

Library of Congress Control Number: 2011902147

Printed in the United States of America

Any people depicted in stock imagery provided by Thinkstock are models,
and such images are being used for illustrative purposes only.
Certain stock imagery © Thinkstock.

This book is printed on acid-free paper.

Because of the dynamic nature of the Internet, any web addresses or links contained in
this book may have changed since publication and may no longer be valid. The views
expressed in this work are solely those of the author and do not necessarily reflect the
views of the publisher, and the publisher hereby disclaims any responsibility for them.

Dedication

This book is dedicated to my direct children, Tammy Lynn Weiser and Joshua Michael Weston. It is written as an expression of my compassion and love for them even though they both have not been directly with me for many years. Both of my natural children are and have been an important part of my life. I have lived for me first and then for them. They also have been through a lot; both being innocent victims of divorce and of a parent that had not been strong enough to be there when they really needed the care and nurturing of a father. Without my love for them, I would not be around to see them grow and mature into the beautiful people that they are today. To both of them I say,

"I AM SORRY THAT I COULD NOT BE STRONGER." "I PRAY THAT GOD HAS AND WILL CONTINUE TO WATCH OVER AND TAKEN CARE YOU BOTH NOW AND IN THE FUTURE."

Remember; always put your life in the hands of God. He is in control of our lives no matter who we are and what we have done. He will never give us more than we can handle. We are saved by His grace and love.

By: PJ (Author 1998)

Author's Commentary

A lot of what you read in this book may seem fictional at first because what had happened is outside of the normal guideline of society but I assure you everything is very true. Some of the names have been changed so no fingers will be pointed to the parties that they represent. Others will be left unchanged.

This book is an autobiography that could also be seen as a self-testimony of major changes that have occurred in my life. Changes that I feel not all get, or want to experience. This might even be looked at as a second chance at life.

For me, I feel a change for the better, because after over 44 years I have finally found my true self. A part of me that had been suppressed for so many years.

My story could be used as a guide for maintaining, picking up the pieces, and salvaging one's life. Also it could be used as a guide not only for Transsexuals and Transgendered people, but also for all individuals who have had a hard time rebuilding their lives after major trauma and hardships.

As a Cross-dresser/Transvestite, and with my Homosexual/Bisexual behavior, I've decided to live my life differently. This part of my life as female. This is why I started to make some major changes in April of 1998.

I was traumatized by three divorces in 1979, 1985, and 1998. The trauma I suffered is of my own doing by not allowing myself to be me. I was afraid, shy, and a very angry individual for many years.

After making a decision to change I became a completely opposite individual. I am very open and now I live my life instead of hiding.

The road I have chosen is not an easy one to toll. Doing what I have been doing (cross-dressing) for over thirty-three years is also not easy to understand. The thing is what I did is not uncommon. Both men and women try on each other's clothing at least one in their lifetime.

I feel that all men and woman should be allowed to express themselves freely and openly in the world we live in today. We are people who have individual needs and beliefs. We should not be ridiculed and judged for what we say or do, no matter how different these ideals are from those around us; as long as we feel that we are being lead by God.

In fact, even today many feel that I am unique but not alone. There are others like myself who choose to live the rest of their lives as another person completely opposite emotionally and physically to the gender that they had been born into and have been living in the past.

Since living as Paulajean (PJ), I have found out that people still are not accepting to the unusual and unknown especially when an individual remains they're self. The problem that exists today is some people discriminate and create hate crimes against people like me because they don't understand me or are threatened sexually. These are the people that need to be educated and need to open their minds. These people also are the ones that love to point fingers and judge everyone when God should only do the judging. Hopefully what you read will help you to avoid some of the pitfalls and down falls that I have experienced firsthand. I was a lost sinner walking in darkness, pain, anger, and prideful. I was found and reborn and saved by the love and blood of Jesus Christ. He is our Savior.

Rebuilding of your life cannot be done completely by yourself. You definitely need the assistance of others. One has to completely want and then reach out for the change and be healed completely. Doing so isn't easy or free.

Today nothing in this world is free. It does take a lot of work, but if you want it bad enough it is worth it. Each time that you rebuild your life, you become stronger. This time for me it is to be the true and free me. This is who I am today, Paulajean Anne Anderson a beautiful, loving, stronger, and caring person.

You too can be saved as I have and become born again. All you have to do is put God in control as the pilot of your life. Then you must become a servant unto Him dedicating your life totally to Him. He knows we all are sinners. That is why God sent His only Son down to earth to die for our sins that we may be saved through His blood.

God gives and guides us through true Healing. Put God back in control of your life and not Satan. Let Him change, mold, and rebuild you. He is our Creator and the Potter who created us in the first place. He knows and can do all.

Remember that God is in control of our lives and in what we say and do no matter what we would like to believe. He knows our faults and will not give us more than we can endure.

"He loved us so much that He sent Jesus His only Son to die for our sins, that we are be saved." (Paraphrased TLB)

"Once He has started a work in you He will be faithful to complete that work." (Paraphrased TLB)

... "Don't be afraid! Speak out! Don't quit! For I am with you and no one can harm you." (Paraphrased TLB)

I hope that you enjoy what you read as much as I have writing it. Peace and God Bless.

By: PJ (Author 1998)

Introduction to a Late Blooming Transsexual

In this book, I talk about what it was like living a life of a lie. For me that was living my life as a genetic male when the true me was and presently has been female. Living as a Transsexual Male-to-Female here in Orange County California can be done. I have proven this by living this way completely from 1998-thru-2003. I still live this life today only now I am post operative and living my life in Texas.

What you are about to read talks about what I have been and still will continue to go through for the rest of my life.

All Transsexuals go through various stages as they transition into their true self whether it is a Male-to-Female (MTF) or a Female-to-Male (FTM). Each of us will progress at a different rate and experience various types of situations. Some of these situations will be very similar and others a lot different. There are guidelines or "Standards of Care" that must be followed before a male or female can have reassignment surgery.

For me when I decided to first come out completely as my true self I was very afraid. Some of the fears that I faced were: fear of being accepted, fear of being beat up, and fear that I might be doing something wrong. I had been a closet cross-dresser for over 33 years and only dared venture out completely dressed in 1998.

Most of the time I would be dressed in woman's clothing when I was at home alone, or I would wear the clothing underneath my own male clothing. This was not easy for me to do because I had been married and my wife's' never knew my complete story. They suspected the dressing because they would find my clothing many times but would never ask me about them.

As I grew older and started to go into puberty I thought that I had come across a lot of the answers. I have had to ask myself some questions.

Am I wrong for trying to help someone? Am I strong enough mentally and physically to really make a difference? Is this person helping himself or herself? Have they become dependent on me? Are they going to make it with everything that has been and will be happening to them? Will they see their next birthday? Do I want to help them anymore? Do I want her to be my roommate in the future? Is she a burden or an example of what could happen to me? Is it in Gods' plan to really help others? Am I feminine enough to feel the emotions she feels? Am I dealing with my emotions? Have I been dealing with them all along? What about me? Am I helping me? Where am I now with my life? What do I really want with my life? Is everything happening according to plan? What about future plan? Which direction am I heading? Is it all going to happen? Is this all reality or a dream? Am I living a fantasy that is not really the true me? Who am I? Male? Female? Who do I feel I am? Male? Female? Am I really one or the other? Who has the answers? Should I interfere with someone else's life or leave it alone? Should I be getting angry for little things or "Not Sweat the Small Stuff? Is my life out of control? Is God in control of my life?

From the above questions you can see that there is a lot going on within my household, with me, and within my life. Trying to answer all of these questions is very ridiculous or might even become overwhelming. To me they also seem this way. So what is the point that I am trying to make? Instead of dealing with everything all at once we should deal with them one at a time as they come and only if we can have some type of control over the outcome. We shall also deal with the "Here and Now," and not dwell on what has happened in the past or what will happen in the future.

For some of us this means taking things, "Day at a Time," sometimes even, "Moments at a Time." This has caused me to be more pessimistic and not so optimistic. For me this is my way of coping. If something good happens you will be surprised instead of depressed. But is this the right way? Who knows? Everyone is different.

In response to this question, for me, the above actions reflect my present state of mind. Not all of you will agree with me. I'm okay with that, because we all are different. Being different is by one of Gods' designs and not ours. To be different is a good trait to have. That is what makes us individual in what we say and do. It is who we are as a person, and not clones or mindless robots.

Throughout our life time we undergo many trials, hardships, and tribulations. I am no different. I have had my share not only living my life as a lie as a male, but also during my transition to becoming a female.

Many Transsexuals experience the same afflictions that I have been and will be experiencing but we tend to handle them at different levels. Some of us do better than others. Again, this relates back to individuality. There are those who never decide to pursue the transition from male-to-female (MTF) or female-to-male (FTM). Instead they live the rest of their lives not understanding why they are unhappy or confused.

For me going through the transition MTF was inevitable. I had been unhappy living, as a male most of my life but was never sure why I was always angry or unhappy. I would experiment even at a young age with my mother's clothing and makeup. Most of this was always hidden for fear of being beaten by my parents or being teased to a point that I would be mocked and hurt. I never knew why I was always so awkward and clumsy. I didn't totally understand what was wrong with me. Even today I still don't have all of the answers to those questions and the confusion of the past.

By: PJ (Author 1998)

The Early Pre-school Years

On December 18, 1953, I was born at Saint Joseph's Hospital in Milwaukee, Wisconsin. During her pregnancy my mother lived with her in-laws. She did not like living this way but for the time being she had no choice. Mom did smoke during the pregnancy, which caused complications when I was born. This complication was me being born early, having lung problems, allergies, and being too small.

Dad was serving his country in the United States Marine Corps and was stationed on a Marine base in Okinawa, Japan. He did not believe that I was his child because he was not there when I was born. He also never really trusted my mom.

Dad denied me being his son to the point that he did not want to come home. It took a lot of convincing on the part of his parents and my mom to prove that I was really his child. They finally ended up convincing him and sent him a baby picture of me to prove it.

After my dad received the picture, he truly did see that I was his baby boy. He decided to have a special picture of me done in silk. When he was discharged from the service he brought this picture home with him along with other souvenirs.

As I was growing up my mom use to tell me many stories that later had an affect on my life. One of these stories is, I was born so small when I was born that I could be put into a mayonnaise jar.

This was not uncommon because I was born premature due to moms' smoking during her pregnancy. I was also born about a month early. She said that my dad's family would compare me to a small Teddy bear. They thought that the comparison was cute and to the point that I received a nickname. That name was, BoBo.

My aunts, uncles, and cousins would always call me this name when they saw me. Others use to call me JoJo or Joey. All of these nicknames I hated and never stuck with me as I was growing up.

As I grew older, I started to completely hate the nicknames BoBo, JoJo and Joey. I also began to hate my real name of Joseph Alexander especially when the name was used in a sarcastic manner or when I did something wrong.

Another story I remember is when I was 2-3 years old I was trying to walk backwards to get away from mom because I did something wrong. I ended up sitting in a scolding hot bucket of water. I did get scolded, but I don't remember even doing it because the incident was so long ago. All I remember is that I was such a klutz that I would be doing stuff like this all of the time.

After my dad was discharged from the service he started working at one of the foundries located in the Milwaukee, Wisconsin area. He still was pretty restless and did not want to settle down to raise his family. He was pretty messed up and brain washed from the Marines so he continued to drink a lot of alcohol.

After work he would go out drinking with his buddies and not come home until late hours in the morning if at all. Sometimes mom even went out looking for him. When she did find him she would gone for long periods of time. This left me neglected.

When dad did come home, he would smell of booze and be very loud. He would always argue and be physically abusive toward my mom.

At the age of 1 or 2 years old I don't remember what these arguments were about. I was just aware that they were happening by the loud noises and screaming that I heard. There was a lot of slamming and hitting of doors and walls.

Dad did other jobs as being a baker, assembler, truck driver, painter, and janitor. By working so hard he was never home to be a nurturing and caring father to his children. As mentioned he still did a lot of drinking and carrying on.

During these various jobs he still would continue to drink and fight with mom. He never was quite sure on what he wanted to do or be or how he was going to manage this family. It was also like if he didn't want to grow up. Dad did not have the education to do anything but manual labor jobs.

The only jobs dad could hang on to where those that were barely above minimum wage. He never truly had a trade other than the skill of baking he learned in the Marines.

Most of these other jobs were mainly manual labor type jobs that required brawn and minimal or no brains. The highest grade that he completed was the eighth grade. He did receive his GED prior to going into the military.

When I was about 2 years old, mom became pregnant again. She found out that she was going to have another little boy. To me, this meant that I was going to become a big brother, something that I knew nothing about. This time mom didn't smoke.

During moms pregnancy dad would continue to beat on, and argue with her. The drinking continued more than ever. Those nine months of pregnancy were hell but went by quickly. This is when my brother Tom was finally born.

After Tom was born my dad still did not change his ways very much. He just kept on drinking with the guys after work. Sometimes mom would have to go out seeking him or would join him again. Other times she would find him in the arms of other woman. Other times when she did join dad, she would find him flirting with other woman and treated her as if she wasn't there.

Dad accepted Tom as being his natural son right away. The reason is because he was back home stateside during Toms' birth. This change in attitude was something I have always been jealous about throughout most of my life.

About 1 1/2 years after Tom was born mom got pregnant again. This time she was to have a baby girl. Now dad and mom were happy because they finally had a girl after three tries. They both wanted a girl to complete their family.

Again dad did not change his ways all that much. He did decide in order to feed this large family and drink, he would have to hold down more than one job. This meant less time at home and more peace for the rest of the family. Everyone was looking forward to the peace.

One thing dad could do is work and work hard. He held down a day job, 2 part time night jobs, and would bid on, and get extra work for the weekends. At times he held down about 3-4 jobs just to get by. Sometimes he would even just take on handyman jobs just for the extra money. Finally, my sister Cheryl Ann was born.

When this event took place, dad was pretty happy. The reality of being a family man finally started to sink in. He began to settle down some. The drinking didn't stop, but it was not getting any worse like it did when Tom was born. It actually even started to decrease a little, which for all of these years was an accomplishment for dad and the family.

Cheryl, Tom, and I grew up together and got along, as well as any typical toddlers would be when they are so close to the same age. Tom and I even played as friends would, as he got little older. We would play games as: cowboys and Indians, war, and army.

When I played with Cheryl I didn't pick on her because she was so small a cute. I even tried to stick up for her most of the time especially when Tom would pick on her.

Mom thought that it was cute to dress Tom and me up in similar outfits. This way she could pass us off as twins even though I was smaller than Tom. We both would even get a lot of the same items during Christmas and birthdays. I think that the cuteness stuck to me in a whole different way as I grew older. This is something I never understood until later in my life.

In moms eyes I was not the perfect healthy little boy that she thought I was. I was born cross-eyed and would continue to walk into things as windows, tables, and glass doors. I also suffered from many household allergies and asthma. Even with these problems she still was a proud doting mother.

Tom had problems of his own. He ended up having Rheumatic Fever with convulsions at a young age. He almost died from this illness several times as a baby and toddler.

Cheryl was basically a healthy little girl. She only suffered from typical childhood colds and an ear infections. At the age of 4 she did have to have tubes put into her ears to drain out the fluid and these worked for her.

In those days procedures like this was not all that unusual. The only other thing that had happened to her was she fell out of our automobile when it was moving during one of our family vacations. She only received minor injuries and bruising.

At the age of 4 ½-5 years old my parents found out that I had to have two surgeries. One was to correct my crossed eyes, and the other was to cut out my tonsils and adenoids to make my breathing better. Tom also had to have his tonsils and adenoids removed. To my parents this meant two large hospital bills again and they weren't quite prepared for these new bills.

Once I had fallen from the bunk bed. Dad was such a cheap scape and thought he could save money he tried to take care of my injuries himself. This is when he put a butterfly stitch with Band-Aids over the area of my left chin that was busted open.

I was too young to understand why and to know if there would be any other scars later in my life. This crazy fix it job caused a permanent scarring that I would have to live with all of my life.

Of course at the age of five years old I had no clue about what was going to happen to me next. All that I knew is that I had stopped crashing into things and had a sore throat. I do remember getting a lot of strawberry ice cream though.

Both of my parents had their share of bills and problems with us kids. We were always sick with one thing or another. They also never really saved or planned for emergencies.

The bills usually were paid late and started to pile up again. These extensive bills, and the way that dad carried on did not make their relationship any easier. In fact, at times their relationship even seemed worse because there was a lot more fighting, hitting, and destruction of property would occur. Most of these were caused by my dad not being able to hold his temper.

I really hated it when mom and dad would fight. Mom would always get the worse end of it, especially when my dad was drinking which was quite often. There was always yelling, screaming, swearing, and the sound of things being slammed around. Dad was always putting his fists through walls and doors or something. Mom would get so beaten up and have to walk out just to survive. This would happen on quite a few occasions and I would be the one chasing after her and I tried to convince her to come back for the sake of us children. Most of the time she would listen to my pleads.

Shortly after I came out of the hospital I would try to be a good son and help my dad. Dad loved it when he got attention, his way and when we helped him when he didn't need it.

He and mom would like to move the bunk beds that we had around a lot. Sometimes the movement would even be from room to room. Other times the movement would be within the same room.

One time I remember when I was helping dad my brother Tom opened a three-way door and knocked over a scolding hot vaporizer on to my leg. The water ended up scolding both of my legs. The incident mainly surprised me and scared the heck out of everyone. The burns were minor so I was treated by mom at home with water and butter. I was lucky there was no major scarring of my legs from the incident.

About six months to a year after I had my surgeries the whole family decided to take a vacation. We were headed for Ohio and then Florida. The purpose of the trip was to visit relatives on my mom's side of the family like her brother, aunts and stepfather. During the trip Cheryl fell out of the moving only to obtain minor injuries.

My mom informs me that my cousin and me were pretty inseparable, especially when we went on the boat rides at an amusement park. We played and enjoyed each others company like 2 sisters would but in this situation I was a boy. Some of the photos that my parents took would show that we were enjoying ourselves and that the family appeared really close.

The photographs that were taken of our immediate family showed Tom, Cheryl, and me getting along very well together. You could see this by the smiles that we were always showing and by the way that we played together. We appeared to be typical happy family with children.

My dad would always have magazines with naked woman bodies sitting around in his and moms' bedroom. When I saw them I would look at them and strip down to where I was naked. I would then put on moms lipstick and fanaticize that I was one of these women and masturbate. This masturbation started at the age of about 5-6 years old. Most of the time I did so when no one was home, busy, or on the sly. A few years after Cheryl's birth, mom became pregnant again. This time she was to have another little boy. His name was going to be Mark.

At the time of Mark's birth my aunt Jenny's youngest became very sick with an infant disease called SIDS and died. I was in the third grade at the time and was asked to be one of the pallbearers.

When I heard the news I was in a daze. It was hard for me to concentrate, realize, and believe what happened. I acted like a zombie and was barely functional. How could this have happened to such an innocent little baby boy? Life is so unfair.

The day of the funeral I was sick with a 102 degree fever and was still at school. I was surprised and even a bit shocked that we were all going to bury this sweet baby.

Due to my state of shock and illness I went through with all of this and never did shed a tear. The rest of my relatives did though as we could hear the tears and wailing from outside the chapel. As I recall this was one of my first experiences with death and dying within my immediate family.

There were many times when we would visit my grand parents. Most of the time when this happened it was for my dad to have a few quick drinks with his dad Joseph John Powalisz, his brothers, and sisters. The would talk of the past and did speak Polish at times so we would not understand them.

As kids would to be so bored with these visits but we did fine because my grandparents always had toys for us to play with. If we were good and behaved we could take one of these toys home with us.

Sometimes I hated it because grandma was so critical verbally and sickly looking. She was always putting down my mom and being bossy for no reason. I would think why does she do this when she is no better herself.

Grandma had Diabetes and would always chew on orange peal rhines without her teeth. Seeing this was completely gross and disgusting. Their place, especially her room always had the smell of these disgusting oranges.

One day my mom was so upset with what my grandma had been saying about her that she had wished her dead. Shortly after the wish was when grandma did die by choking on an orange peal. Grandpa could not save her, but the suspicion is that he didn't even try. This was a completely weird and spooky coincidence.

After grandma died our house doorbell started to ring all by itself even after being disconnected from the electrical current. When that happened everyone was starting to freak out. This is when my mom regretted her wish. She started to pray for the noise to stop. Eventually it did after several hours. It was as it grandma's spirit was finally at rest.

Dad thought that this incident was an omen or something. He hated mom for wishing his mom dead. In fact, the whole incident was repeated many times during the arguments that my parents had.

We buried grandma within that same week. Again I did not shed any tears because I truly never cared for grandma. This was my second experience with death in our family.

The rest of the family remained solemn and quiet. They didn't morn over grandma like they did with my aunt Jenny's baby. I think that most of them also hated grandma and were glad to see her gone.

During the next few years I remember witnessing a lot more cruelty in our home. My dad would yell at and beat on my mom more and more each day. He was torn and devastated by his mom's death. My way of ignoring everything was to escape from the stress was to go back into my fantasy of being a woman and masturbating. This is when I cross-dressed using my mom's clothing.

One time my mom just had to leave and ended up walking several miles on her own. I know this because I was the one who followed her all of the way and tried to persuade her to come back home. She would tell me that she hated dad for everything he has been doing to bring the family down. During this walking she would try to release some of her own anger by venting or talking to those around her. This time it was me that she shared her feelings with. Eventually she would give in to my pleas. When this would happen dad would become very apologetic and came to pick me and her up. The kindness would last for a day or so. After this amount of time he would then start in on her all over again with his abuse.

When dad would not only pick on mom, he would start turning on us kids. To avoid being picked on I had to learn at an early age to keep my mouth shut. I didn't want to be the brunt of my dad's wrath. When I did fight back he threatened to kill me with his bare hands. After that incident I completely lost respect for him. At other times it was better to just stay out of the way. For me this was my way of surviving the inevitable.

As I already mentioned, one of my ways with dealing with my feelings during this time was to dress up in mom's undergarments as a bra, underwear, hose, and shoes. I would even experiment with the lipstick and eyeliner pencil.

While dressed like this I would masturbate as I fantasized that I was a woman. I would hide in a locked room and do so. None of my family ever new about this at the time.

In time it ended up that not only dad was involved in abusing us kids. Mom also would get involved only to get herself hurt one way or another.

Most of the time her injuries were caused by one of us blocking her hits or the awkwardness of her being the aggressor. This was not her best role with us kids.

Tom was different when he dealt with mom and dad. He would speak his mind and stand up to both of them at the same time. He would even loose control and yell back at them. Most of the time this was done for attention but mom and dad did not like it. Other times it was because he was totally fed up with it all abuse, noise, and crap that was going on. Of course these behaviors is why he would always be in trouble.

Cheryl had it made. As the only girl she was the apple in dad's eye. She was never in trouble or picked on by him. Boy how I envied her so. I wanted that attention she received.

The Elementary School Years

My first years of school started out rocky. I had not had my eye surgery yet so I still kept running into things. With my eyes this way I also could not read, make out a lot of the letters of the alphabet or write yet. All of this slowed me down significantly but I was still passed through Kindergarten anyway. Finally after having the corrective surgery I started to see things a lot better.

By the time I entered into the First Grade I still could barely make out the alphabet and print my name yet. In fact, I was so slow at learning that the counselors, teachers, and my mom decided to hold me back a semester because I was so far behind and had trouble catching up. When this happened I was devastated. I could not understand why all of this was happening to me. I also decided at this young age of 6 years old that I would get that semester back one way or another even if it meant dropping out of school later on in my life.

Both of my parents did not like the Public School system in Milwaukee, Wisconsin, so they decided to send all of us to a private Catholic School for grades 1-8. To do so this meant that mom would have to also work. We would do Kindergarten in the Public School and then transfer to a Catholic School.

The first Catholic school that I recall attending was at Saint Barbara's. This school was about four to six blocks from where we lived on 32nd Street. At first we would get a ride to school. By the time we knew the way, we were told to start doing the walk to school ourselves.

The walk home from school usually took about fifteen to thirty minutes. If it took longer than that mom would start to ask us why. She would really drill us until we answered her and it had better been the truth because she would always call the school sometimes before we would get there.

The next Catholic school that we transferred to was Saint Adelberts. This school was about three to four miles from where we lived. Again mom started to drive us each morning, but that didn't last very long either. She had us walking again by the middle of winter. The walk was at least 4-5 miles and about 1 1/2-to-2 hours to walk depending on the traffic and the route we took.

During the winter this walk became very cold. We had to really bundle up warm or we would have frozen to death. This is when I began to dread getting up early enough to do this walk each day. I knew if I poked around mom would eventually drive me. Sometimes when I walked I ended up having some other problems.

Just before I made it to school I would have episodes of stress incontinence of either urine or movement of my bowels. This would usually happened more often when I was sick. If I had an accident, I would either have to sit in it all day in school, or walk home and change. Most of the time I ended up going back home because I was to embarrassed to go to school wet or dirty.

When I did go back home mom would help to get me cleaned up and ready for school again. She would also drive me back to school so I wouldn't be very late.

These incidents made me late for school but they did not happen very often. After about a year of doing these walks mom finally decided that it would be better for her to just drive us since we lived so far. Eventually we moved to within two to three blocks of this school. When this happened my problem was no longer an issue. Neither was the walking.

By the time I was in the Third Grade we had been going to this school for over a year. Mom decided that she wanted Tom and I to become alter boys and to get involved with Cub Scout activities. This meant that Tom and I had to learn the Mass Celebration in Latin and attend scout meetings at least once a week.

Latin was a hard language for me to learn. I think that the reason I had so many problems is because I already behind in my reading and writing. I also think that the other part of the problem is I had an undiagnosed learning disability.

I just couldn't catch on to then correct a annunciation, punctuation, and spelling of the words. Tom had no problems learning this new language because he was very studious and smarter than I was.

Mom had to work with me for hours until I had the correct sounds for the words and had memorized the complete alter boy portion of the Mass Celebration. Once I understood this portion, I chose to listen closer to the priest portion and taught myself his part. This is when I discovered that I could teach myself something new once I had the hang of how the language worked. Once I learned something I could memorize it for use in the future. As mentioned I did finally catch on and became involved with assisting the priest during his services.

One time I was selected as one of the twelve apostles during a High Mass at the Easter Ceremony. The Arch Bishop washed our feet, as a symbol of what Jesus Christ did at prior to His Last Supper with the true twelve apostles.

During this service Confirmation candidates received the Sacrament of Confirmation. I was one of these candidates.

Besides being an active alter boy I really got involved with the Cub Scouts. I would go to meetings at least once a week. After working with Tom and I, mom decided to get a part time job. Later this job became full time as a teachers aid.

During the summer I learned how to play baseball. I wasn't a very good athlete, but at least I tried and did get better with practice. Some of these activities were fun but were to strenuous for me. Other times they were boring but in all I always learned something new from most of the scout meetings and the ball games.

Mom was as hard a worker as my dad was so she had no problems finding a job. She also could type about 120 words per minute and almost had her associates degree.

Her first job was as a Teachers Aid at one of the local Public Schools. She did this until she was able to land a position as an Administration Clerk with the Public School System. In time she became pretty good at her job.

During the summer my brother Tom, Cheryl and me learned about collecting newspapers, cardboard, cans, and rags. We would turn them in for extra spending money. Mom or dad would take what we collected to the junkyard for us. Sometimes we would fill the Catalina Station wagon up completely and had to make several trips. This is how we bought our first real big bicycles. Making our own money made us proud because we could choose any type of bicycle that we wanted and our parents had no say in the matter.

Both of my parents loved to have us working hard doing this kind of work. They figured that they weren't to proud to earn money this way so why should we be. The sad part is there were times when we would not see any of the money because mom and dad would keep it. They said that the money would be used to feed us kids. A lot of times that was a total lie. It was used for dads booze.

Because I was very different from the boys in the neighborhood I was always getting into fights with the boys in our new neighborhood. I was still somewhat klutzy so I would not participate in the football and baseball games as often as Tom. Instead I would stay pretty much to myself and continue with my cross-dressing and fantasies.

By the time I was in the Seventh Grade I started to get too old for the Cub Scouts. Mom and dad enrolled Tom and I into the Boy's Club. They felt that this was an inexpensive way of keeping us out of their hair for a few hours during the night. Of course their plan worked.

By this time Tom and I really became involved with the Boy's Club. We participated in all kinds of sports and activities. Here are some of the activities we did.

Tom played a lot of basketball, football, gym hockey and other sports. I learned woodcraft, poetry, swimming, track, writing, and Indian Lore. When I did become involved in sports it was things like inner track events as the long jump, high jump, shot put, and throwing the javelin.

Tom was always better than me in these types of sports. Again this had caused a lot of jealousy on my part. I was so darn competitive but truly didn't have the endurance and strength to do very well.

The first year with the Boy's Club Tom and I both did earn a sweater letter and our first trip to a Boy's Club Camp. I earned it from my crafts and writing. He earned it from his sports. Sometimes I think that the counselors just felt sorry for me, and this is how I have felt most of my life.

Tom stuck to his sports. For some reason he was good at any type of sport he tried. I envied that part of him as much as I envied my sister who received a lot of attention from my parents.

At camp I became involved in the crafts again. I learned to work with leather, beads, and feathers. I actually became very creative and skilled especially when it came to doing leather goods and with working with wood.

I felt as though that I was a true full pledged Indian Buck in training to become a Brave. I thought that being one with nature caused me to have a lot of good feelings instead of my gender dysphonic ones. This was another way of living out a fantasy but at a different level.

I learned how to live off the land, about plants that can be used for food, and things that our ancestors, (the Indians) did when they where the main people living in this country of ours. To me all of this was the history of our land and interesting. I absorbed what I could like a sponge.

While at camp I decided to work on earning my Indian Ranks, which was one of the perks that the camp had to offer. My goal was to complete all of the ranks that I could as quick as possible and maybe even become an Indian Chief before I couldn't go to camp again.

I took to the earning of my Indian Ranks just as I did with everything else. All out and in a "Gun Ho Manner." I also did the same with working on my crafts. I did well enough to teach others.

During the fall of this same year I started to attend Indian Lore group meetings called the IN-DA-WIN-DA-WIN Society. This group would have weekly meetings and would actually go out and entertain for disabled people in Skilled Nursing Homes in Milwaukee, Wisconsin and surrounding areas. They didn't do this for money, but as a way of helping others. I loved it when I could go with them. It gave me the opportunity to show off what I have been learning and I was an active participate with a group that seemed to care and help others. By being in these costumes I was able to show off my legs and wear ribbons on silk and thing in public without being embarrassed.

When I told mom about what I was doing and what the group did, she was very supportive. In fact, she helped me to make a costume completely out of silk and ribbon. We tried to use one of the designs I found from the Indian Lore books I would always bring home from the library.

While making this costume mom and I became a little closer. I watched her attentively as she buzzed through the silk material on her sewing machine. By watching her I learned to sew by hand, a trait that would stay with me the rest of my life.

Mom shared with me that my interest in Indians came from her side of the family and the Indian blood I had in me. I really enjoyed what I heard and we became even closer. I enjoyed having this quality time with mom. I just missed this same kind of time with my dad.

The following year I earned my letter again and away I went to camp. While there I started to continue to work more in Indian Crafts building and learned more advanced ways to work with wood, leather, beads, and feathers. I took what I learned and started to teach the younger children. The crafts counselor saw what I was doing and took me under his wing because I truly showed an interest in the kids. Also by me working with them his job was a whole lot easier.

These kids were eating up the teaching like sponges. For me hands on teaching was becoming actually a lot of fun. After a few sessions with these kids I even asked the Director if I could help him more often. He let me become his assistant for the summer.

Another thing I liked about what I was doing at camp is the ability to experience nature. I would love to run through the woods in nothing but shorts, a T-shirt, and moccasins. Some times I would even run through the woods partially naked. Doing so made me feel as one with nature.

There were other times I would have the fantasy that I was really one of the Indians of the past. This fantasy to me was also a lot of fun and would always stay with me especially at camp.

That year I earned two more ranks. Now was an Indian Brave with the Indian name of "Black Bear." The meaning of this name is, "One of Great Strength and a Brother of Nature." This name was given to me because of the karma, aura of nature that surrounded me, and because I was so good with working with the younger kids. I tried to live up to this name during the rest of that summer.

By the time winter had come along I was a candidate for becoming a member of the IN-DA-WIN-DA-WIN Society. I attended all of their meetings and even was able to go to Winter Camp with them. The group adopted me as one of them and I really continued to finally blossom into a real full pledged member.

By spring we found out that the Milwaukee Arena wanted to have a major "Folk Lore" event. Groups of people from all over the world were to participate. The Boy's Club's in Milwaukee were invited to participate. For Milwaukee this was a major event.

Our group was asked to be part of it since we represented the Irving Boy's Clubs there in the city. For us this event was a major one and meant that finally we would be involved in something we liked to do. It also meant a lot of work and practice.

For the "Folk Lore" event we decided to do Free Style Dancing (or showing off of our dancing style), The Ribbon Dance (the demonstration of basket weaving and unweaving), and The Horse Tail Dance (or how a white stallion has control over a herd of horses). One of us was going to do the Hopi Hoop Dance (which showed how an Indian could dance and work with hoops). We had to these dances down cold in a very short amount of time mainly because they were very common to us.

The "Folk Lore" event went off without a glitch. We participated in it for about three days. It was great and an experience I will always remember it because to me it was fun to do. Mistakes were made during some of these dances but nobody cared because we had fun doing it.

After this experience I really felt like part of the group and a real Indian. I was part of something important that made a difference. We also were exposed to the public since we were on local television channel and paper. At the end of the event we even celebrated with cookies and juice. Besides being involved with this Indian Lore group I remained active in the Boy's Club.

Towards the end of the summer the work I was doing at camp was not unnoticed. I made the rank of Medicine Man and finally the rank of Chief, because I knew that this was going to be my last summer here at camp. As a Chief I completely ran the last Indian Ceremony of the summer. Hardly anyone attended so the ceremony ended up being a big flop. The thing is I didn't care because the attitude of the director's and the kids were changing.

Until this point I still was a pretty normal boy except for my cross-dressing and gay behaviors which I tried to keep hidden.

There were times when I was really confused about my gender identity. I experienced most of this confusion, as I was experiencing puberty. These questions would always haunt me. "Am I an all American boy or a girl in a boys' body? Who am I? At this point I felt that only time would tell.

By this time mom and dad decided that it was time to change churches again. For us kids this meant that we could end up doing a lot of walking to school again. This time it was only 2 miles one way.

Around this same time I had experienced my first homosexual experience. An older boy asked me to join him in the boy's bathroom. He asked me to take off all of my clothes and join him in one of the empty bathroom stalls. At first I thought this would be a rape, but I went with the flow and I ended up liking the thought that I could finally truly live out my fantasy.

I was still naive at so I did join him for fear that he would possibly beat me up. Of course that never happened. He then asked me to sit on his lap naked and play with his penis, which I did without hesitation. He was getting an erection in my hands.

I had never seen anything like this before other than when it happened with myself when I wore moms' and my sister Cheryl's clothing. I continued to help him masturbate but he could not come to a climax but he was really becoming turned on. I was even becoming somewhat aroused myself. From the bathroom we both went swimming butt naked.

While in the pool he had me play with his penis again and asked me to suck on it while under water. I tried to but could not hold my breath long enough to do what he asked. He later took me back to the bathroom and I did suck and kiss his penis until he climaxed. I made sure that I licked up every drop.

I found by this experience that I actually didn't mind sucking, kissing, playing with another guys penis, scrotum, and balls. I also didn't mind swallowing semen if I had too. From this point on I knew that my sexual life had become more confusing to me. I started to feel out of place and enjoyed being with and doing a guy sexually.

I didn't know what it was like to be with a female yet. I was still as much a virgin in this area as I was with my gay experiences. I knew that time would come in the future to experience being with a female though.

My parents never found out about this incident. I was not about to tell on myself or talk about it, especially since I decided later that I did enjoy the situation. I have learned from my brother's mistakes and continued to keep things to myself and keep my mouth shut.

Shortly after this event I decided to experiment more for myself. I would gather up some more of my sisters' and moms' clothes. These would include some heels and makeup, a bra, panties, tights, and sometimes dresses or skirts.

When I dressed in this apparel again I would fantasize more about being a woman. I would also gratify my fantasy by masturbating pretending that I was at the receiving end of intercourse instead of giving it. I enjoyed these feelings a lot because they did make me feel like I was being loved. I usually did these acts in one of the large closets or a large vacant room in our house.

For me dressing in woman's clothing and hiding had become a real turn on. I enjoyed the risk I took possibly getting caught. I loved the fantasy and it relieved a lot of my stress.

At times I also loved to put on my sister's clothes and pretend I was her twin. This happened especially when I stayed in her room while she was away. My parents and the rest of the family never knew and for me that was fine.

One time while I was dressed in the large closet my brother Tom came in on me. He caught me dressed in tights, heels, makeup and everything and asked me what I was doing. I had to think fast so I lied to him. I told him that I was trying to put together a costume for Halloween. I was going to go as Catwoman. He told me that I looked ridiculous and that mom had been calling for me for a while.

I quickly changed our of these clothes and answered mom's call. To this day I don't think that Tom has shared what he saw me doing with the rest of the family. I would continue to intermittently have episodes where I would cross-dress in this large closet or in other rooms throughout the house but I became more cautious about it.

Of course with the change of schools comes the making of new friends. For me making new friends was not an easy task. I was the new kid on the block and I started off by being picked on by a lot of the bigger guys. I was always in a fight one way or another. My being gay didn't help matters either. In fact, I think that being gay could even have been why I was picked on.

I ended up getting my lips busted open several times requiring stitches, getting black eyes, and a lot of hurt muscles. I also ended up being a follower instead of a leader. The main reason is because it was a lot easier that way and that meant fewer fights. I also think a lot of this happened because I was a bit of a sissy.

When I was at school I would imitate a lot of the other guys by dressing and walking like them. To me this was my way of trying to be cool. Of course this was hard to do though when what I would have rather warn was a pretty dress with silk, lace, with hose and being made up like the other girls. So much for trying to fit in.

I hated the clothes my parents bought me so I decided that if I wanted certain things as different clothes that I needed to get a job to buy them for myself. I bought most of my men's clothing and continued to use my mom's and sister's clothing for my cross-dressing (which continued hidden of course). There were times I would buy my own woman's shoes but that was less frequent. I ended up doing all of this by getting a paper route and really learned the business.

I got pretty good at delivering the papers on time and worked myself up to the largest route in the station. This was a lot of work, but around Christmas time it was well worth it. My customers really liked me and gave me all kinds of extra money and gifts. I made out like a bandit.

As you can see by now I was a pretty busy guy. I worked, went to school, and was still active with the Boy's Club. I was hardly at home, which for me was a good thing. The temptation of cross-dressing was less dominate in my life but was still happening.

When I dressed, I wanted to be in these clothes all of the time. I didn't think that any of my family would understand. I wasn't sure that I completely understood why either.

While being with the group of boys I hung around, I was not the best boy either. I learned to drink alcohol, smoke marijuana, lie, smoke cigarettes, cheat, swear, fight, steal, and even vandalize. I became a regular hoodlum and gangster. After some time I finally learned to defend myself better. I was in more fights, was doing bodybuilding at the Boys Club, and learned about boxing.

If I brought my gangster ways home with me I would be in trouble, especially with my dad who was still drinking the way he does.

I hated having to even deal with dad at all. To me he was a poor excuse of a man and a very poor example for his children to follow. Due to his abuse of my mom and us I no longer respected him.

None of these feelings was right in any means. It may have been my way of rebelling against life, my family, and my confusion about my sex role in life. Who knows what drove me?

During the last part of the eighth grade I started to skip class and drink wine with some of the guys. They dared me to rip off the local Donut Shop. I did so and was dared to throw a pie at one of the girls. I took this dare also and got in trouble for both.

On rainy days we would hide out in the boy's bathroom and give each other pink bellies with a rough hairbrush. When we did this it made so much racket, that then nuns (we called them penguins because their habits looked like those of a penguin in a suit) would hunt for us. We also would smoke in that bathroom and go to drink at a friend's house.

One time we were threatened by one of theses nuns. She said she would call us on the carpet and call our parents if we kept up with our nonsense. We shined her on because we knew that she couldn't prove anything. She never did follow through on her idle threats.

Also while in the eighth grade I was still an alter boy but not a very good one. I would drink the wine for the Mass Celebration and steal from the collection box. I figured that since my classmates did it, why shouldn't I.

One night I was supposed to be serving for a night Mass Celebration. Instead of doing so I decided to skip it and went out with some friends. We went driving around town with some girls. By the time that the night was over we eventually ended up going bowling.

I stayed gone later than usual and lied about it. The problem is my mom had checked up on me and found out I had lied to her. She covered for me because my dad was not home from work yet. She also knew if dad found out I would be in serious trouble.

Mom would cover for us a lot. This time I promised her I wouldn't lie to her again. I also thanked her for watching out for me.

By the time of my graduation from the eighth grade, I decided to have a party. A bunch of us got together and tried to form a group. I played a guitar but very poorly. The guys still used me because I was part of their click. The party turned out pretty bad.

Another time a group that was forming a band asked me to come over and try out as a singer. I did not have much experience, but I went for it anyway. The song of their choice was "Black Magic Woman" by Santana. When I sang the song, the group said that it sounded great except that I didn't know the words or the cues on when to start singing. They worked with me for about an hour and then gave up on me because I just was not getting it. I was told that I sounded just like the original singer of the song. So much for my singing career in a band.

The High School Years
-1968

I finally graduated out of grade school and the eighth grade. I was beginning to start high school in the fall. This meant another full summer at camp. This time I worked as a maintenance helper. That didn't last very long because I was pretty lazy and still had my problems with catching on to a lot of things. I was able to help out with the crafts though. By the end of the summer I became an assistant cabin counselor

After school started I was in less trouble than before. I think that this was because I had to adjust to a new setting and surroundings consisting of new friends, policies to follow, and rules. Don't get me wrong. I also was no angel either. I still worked and because I was working, I showed my parents that I was more responsible. This is why I was allowed to go out more. I still did my cross-dressing but it was less frequent.

My respect for my dad was becoming a joke. I no longer cared about what happened with him. He could have dropped dead drunk for all I cared.

I became very self centered and selfish. I would do what I wanted to do no matter what, good or bad. Most of the time it was bad, but I learned a way to get away with things which was to be sly and sneaky about. With my folks that was not very hard to do.

An example of this is when I even ripped off a simpleminded and a handicapped individual that owned a Thrift Store in our neighborhood. I did this with the help of a friend. Later I felt guilty so I turned myself in and tried to make it up to the guy. He ended up being okay about my apology.

While in the ninth grade my feminine side started to show more often in a different manner than being totally dressed as a woman. I started to like to wear loud and bright clothes in many different styles and colors. Sometimes I would even wear woman's tennis shoes, blouses, hose, and calf high laced up boots not only at home but also to school under my male clothing. No one ever noticed or even cared.

Due to the way that I was dressing I earned the nickname of "Pajama Man" or "PJ for short." This nickname stuck with me throughout high school. It was even mentioned and printed in my yearbook in 1972 the year I graduated.

I still participated with the Boy's Club, Camp, and my paper route. My hoodlum ways did not change at all. I cheated on exams, would sell my homemade lunches, vandalize the lunchroom, drink, and gamble. I always was in trouble and fights one way or another.

After finishing the ninth grade I made it to another summer at Camp. Here is where I learned to drive my first stick or standard shift truck. The experience for me was great. I also learned more about what marijuana was.

We would party by bringing beer into our quarters and smoking pot, which was against camp policy. A lot of nights we would do all nighters. By the time I was in the tenth grade I was starting to be noticed as a troublemaker and not as a "Newby" or "Freshie," but also as one of the guys. I remember to me it finally felt good to fit in.

One time when my brother had just started the ninth grade and some guys in the lunch room started picking on him. They didn't like him because he was so smart and athletic. I didn't like others picking on him or what I saw so I jumped over a couple of table's and started a fight. I grabbed one of the guys who was picking on him and put him in a headlock almost choking him to death. This all happened so fast that I didn't care what would happen to me. I just wanted to make sure my brother was safe at the time.

I didn't want to let off of the guy. When all of this commotion ended I was expelled for three days. Mom again covered for me because I stuck up for Tom (my brother). Dad was even proud of me because I stood up for my brother and he told me so.

The more new friends I met the worse things got for me. I started to do other things as drinking and smoking cigarettes more often. I found out that I had a taste for Rum & Coke, Whiskey, Gin, and eventually acquired the taste for wine and beer, smoking marijuana, and cigarettes.

Sometimes during our lunch all that I would do is drink. Half the time I would finish my classes for the rest of the day half plastered. This was easy since I really didn't eat very much lunch.

I planned my schedule to the point that my last classes would be shop. The Aviation Shop had a lot of places to hide and drink. It also was easy to distract our teacher so we took turns doing so.

While in shop I also gambled by flipping quarters against others. Sometimes I would do pretty well and knew to quit while I was ahead. We also drank alcohol in the bathroom all of the time.

By the end of my sophomore year I held down other odd jobs and finally gave up my paper route. On the weekends I would go out dancing. Mom would drop me off and of course I would get a ride home. This being dropped off only happened once in a while. I later learned to take the bus until I received my driver's license.

While at the dances I would mingle with a tough crowd of guys from the same part of town I was from. I even became part of a gang of Polish kids from the south side of town (where I lived). When we would meet it would be early to drink down some whiskey or rum. After drinking our share we would figure out who we would start a fight with that night. Most of the time our fights would be with Mexicans. If the fighting was not physical it would be out on the dance floor.

I would carry my dad's Marine bayonet. He never used it and I figured it wouldn't missed. It never was. I also never used it because it was just for show.

Usually every dance ended up in a fight. When we weren't fighting our group would hog up the dance floor by doing dances as the twist, mash potatoes, funky chicken, the swim, the swing, and the hustle. I always thought that the bands that we saw were cool. Of course as I was growing up a lot of new bands were just getting started.

A lot of times we were able to see multiple bands battling it out to see who was the best. This was called; "Battle of the Bands." I was able to see the beginnings of bands as; Chicago, Santana, and Freddy and the Freeloaders. One of the band members was even a neighbor of mine. Another group had three of my cousins in it.

At one of these dances I thought I met my first real girlfriend. I remember her name being Sheila Sexton. I figured she was cool and experienced. Maybe she even lived up to her last name ("Ton of Sex"- Sexton).

We got along pretty well at first, but in the end we did break it off. Part of the reason was because my folks didn't like her and where she lived (which was West Allis) was quite a distance from me. I didn't want to break it off with her, but having hindsight I know it was for the best. She was a big tease and I was still so naive I went for all of it. I was crushed. This just added to my already present sexual identity crisis.

At the age of fifteen years old I was able to get into most bars without getting carded. This was a new scene for me and I liked it. I also was able to order drinks which of course I did many times.

The reason I was not carded is because of the way that I acted, dressed, and I had a full grown mustache. I found that it helped sometimes to look and act older than you are, especially when you wanted to drink. I finished off the year by meeting other girls at bars and the Veterans hospital.

During the beginning of my junior year I continued to go to dances. I also became a member of an Elite group called; "The Host Club". The group was for students that held a GPA of a 3.0 or better. I made it into this group by cheating on some of my courses and buckling down on my studies. I knew that I could maintain a 3.0 when I buckled down, didn't drink, and stayed out of trouble. If you noticed, so far I was always the one that took and looked for short cuts.

Again during this same year I held down odd jobs when I wasn't involved with school activities. Part of the reason is because I started hitting the booze more just like my dad had been doing during all of my life. One of these jobs was as a baker's helper. It lasted only a short amount of time because I began to hate cleaning up baker messes. They are such slobs with the flour, sugar, and batters. From there I did a couple other janitorial jobs. They weren't as bad but this was not what I wanted to do the rest of my life and I knew it. I also realized that this was the only type of work I could do since I was just a student in high school. I knew that I should not have to kill myself to earn an almighty buck by using my brawn like my dad. I felt that I was a lot smarter and far better than he was because I was educated. This is why I decided to try to use my brain. This same year I finally learned to drive.

I was a terrible driver and kept having accidents all of the time. When I had these accidents I lied about them for fear of being beat up by my dad and not being able to drive anymore. I also didn't tell him I was drinking and driving when some of these accidents occurred. I knew that he would kill me if I told him.

I remember my dad was getting worse with his drinking and cruelty to my mom. I hated it but knew for now I couldn't do anything about it for the purpose of my own temper and survival. When he tried to spank me once I ended up laughing in his face and yelled back threatening him. I don't think that he ever handled that incident well because he has hated me ever since.

After dad was done beating up on mom he would always want to wrestle with us.

At a young age I played along with it but as I got older I hated it. I remember that when he was this way (being totally drunk), that he would get a little to rough with his horseplay.

One of these times I didn't want any part of it so I started to strike out at him. He didn't realize the anger that I was holding in when I fought back and I did get some good hits in. I think I got a couple good hits to his face because he just blew up and used his weight and strength to pin me against the wall threatening to kill me if I ever struck back at him again. This made me angrier with him and I tried to stay out of his way for fear of my life. I was about 15 or 16 years old at the time that this happened. I lost total respect for him from this point on.

I knew that I would be scarred for life and never forget this incident. This scarring would just add to the scarring I have already experienced witnessing him hitting my mom all of those years.

By my senior year I just decided that I had enough with school, dad, jobs, and life. I decided to keep drinking almost every day for days at a time. My cross-dressing problem was happening more frequently but was still hidden. I just didn't care anymore about anything. Many times I would even play hooky just for kicks.

I still would go to my dances as I had been doing the past few years. I even met someone at one of these dances. Her name was Sue and she was flirting with me. I found myself attracted to her. I was seventeen years old at the time.

One day we both played hooky together so I ended up coming over to her house. She let me in and we started off kissing. From kissing we moved to petting. I was getting totally turned on. I could not control myself anymore so I totally undressed her. This was a new experience for me so I was a bit clumsy. I did not want to stop. She resisted at first so I ended up forcing myself on her and raped her. In time it didn't feel like rape to her. She started to enjoy it as much as I did. Shortly after this incident we found we couldn't keep our hands off each other. We went to booze parties, football games, and other dances. I even took her to one of the main parks and almost totally raped her right there in the park.

After some time we got caught and I ended up lying my way out to a policeman by saying I didn't understand English in Spanish. The cop let us off. We decided at this point that fucking in public was not the best idea especially after just being caught.

Since I couldn't keep my hands off this girl I decided to look for the opportunity to be with her when mom and dad weren't home and when I could. Even when they were home we would go to the vacant front bedroom or my sister's room or in the poolroom in our basement. My little brothers were very naive and had no clue on what we were doing. We both didn't care; we just did what we wanted to do anyway.

One time I had another party at the house when mom and dad were gone. The party was busted up by my parents early because of the drinking and smoking of Oreginal. My dad even mocked me by trying to smoke Oreginal himself.

This kind of stuff seemed to happen a lot during the eight to twelve weeks or so that I dated this girl. To tell the truth as I already mentioned I didn't care. Also the thing is she was not the girl that I wanted to be with. I wanted her older sister who was slimmer and prettier. We finally did break it all off. She felt that she had found someone else and because we were being too sexual (or so I thought).

At this point now I was completely confused. I just wanted to be with anything in a skirt. I didn't care if I was on the receiving end or doing it myself. I went for girls three to six years younger than me, especially if they were cute and had any type of figure. I wanted sex all of the time. Being almost eighteen most of these girls were jail bait for me.

One time I even took one of these younger girls to a homecoming dance knowing that it was the wrong thing to do. My parents told me that I better watch myself because I could end up in jail for rape. The younger girl thing only lasted about six months or so. I then returned to my drinking, cross- dressing, and masturbating.

The last week of school prior to Christmas break I played hooky a lot more than usual. Most of the time I went drinking with my friends. This happened most of the time during my lunch hours. After school I landed a job as a shoe salesman thinking that this is what I wanted to be. I blew the job off by going into work totally wasted, drunk, and smelling like alcohol. I was so plastered that I got sick on the job with the dry heaves. I sold my first pair of shoes but I threw up (or barfed) on the customer's shoes right after closing the sale. I continued to get sick all of the way running to the bathroom. I remained this way for about an hour into my shift. I eventually ended up going home, but only after I cleaned up the mess that I had made. I could have continued to work for the company but was too embarrassed from the episode that I just quit the job.

On the last day of school, which was close to my eighteenth Birthday, I was invited to a friend's house. He had bought me a fifth of Bourbon hoping that I would open it and share it with him. Of course I did not let him down. We started off light at first by mixing the Bourbon with cokes. By the time we had three drinks each we were having the Bourbon straight.

Boy were we ever plastered. I was so plastered in fact that I was very obnoxious and rude towards my friend's mother. I even became loud, threatening, and rowdy. I was so bad that I started to blow off steam and cussed her out not knowing that she would call the police on me. I ended up going to jail that night to sleep the alcohol off. I did not want my folks called because I didn't want them to see me like this. Deep down I also knew that I might say things to them I might regret later.

When released from jail in the morning I was pissed off with everything and at everyone, especially my parents. I was also very hung over.

By this time Tom was already put into Juvenile Hall for mouthing off to my dad. I just wanted out and had to figure out how to get out and away from everything but I had to have a plan. What I decided to do was close out my savings account and move out on my own. I was so out of it and depressed that I also decided that I was fed up with school.

Since the beginning of high school I had been monitoring all of my high school units. I knew up until this point I had finished enough units to graduate a semester early. This is when I decided I was going to try to pursue that route.

Soon after I moved out I decided to isolate myself. I could not hold back from being myself any longer. I had it all planned out. I was going to try to live out my fantasy of being a female and starting a new life.

My folks did get worried and started looking for me. It took a long time for them to find me but they did. This was only after I called them to let them know I was going to get the rest of my clothes later on in the week.

When I was found I tried to let them know that if I came home that it would only be on a temporary basis. I still wanted out. They decided to help me to get into the military. For me this was my only way out since life at home was so bad.

You're In The Army Now
-1972

By this time it is January of 1972. My draft number for the mandatory draft into the military was 13. I decided instead of being drafted that I would volunteer. I thought that enlisting was better than being placed into a branch of service I didn't like, or being sent to Viet Nam against my own will.

Getting indoctrinated into the military was not an easy task. Actually it was very involved and complicated. Part of this was because I had decided to drop out of school without my high school diploma. This meant taking a test to get my General Education Diploma (GED). Also the only branch of service that I wanted to be in was the United States Army instead of the Marine Corps that my dad had been in. I felt that I was still way better and smarter than him so why repeat his stupidity and become brain washed.

The recruiter was great with working with me. He set up a time and place for me to take the GED exam. He even drove me to Madison, Wisconsin for the exam and made sure that I would be picked up after I was done.

I did take the GED exam cold turkey without preparation. For me this was not the way to take tests since I already have a reading and learning deficit. I ended up failing the exam miserably. Because of this, I was scheduled to take it again in thirty days, which for me was too long for me to hang around home. I hated it that much.

This is when I decided to check with my high school counselor to see if there were any alternatives. I knew from following my schedules for the past 3 1/2 years that I had already completed enough units to graduate. I just wanted him to make sure that I was right.

When checking with the guidance counselor I discovered that I was correct and that I would be able to graduate with a General Education High School Diploma (the same degree given by the GED exam.

I started to out-process from the school and completed it in one day. I then went back to my Recruiter and was indoctrinated into the Army within the month.

By this time Richard Nixon decided to start pulling troops out of Viet Nam. I was to start off my military career by being assigned to Fort Ord, California. From there I would be assigned to Fort Carson, Colorado for Armor Tank training.

There were three of us leaving from Milwaukee, Wisconsin to Fort Ord, California. I felt at least I would not be totally alone during the trip. I tried to make friends fast.

Immediately after being sworn into the Army we were put up in a sleazy hotel and given a meal ticket for the night meal. This was at the Army's expense of course. The thing is I couldn't sleep so I laid in my room naked and masturbated. This helped me relieve the stress I was feeling all day and month. I figured who would know and for that matter care what I did.

Our flight was to leave early in the morning. I wasn't sure that I really wanted to go along with all of this, but I thought to myself that doing this is better than the crap that I had been experiencing at home. I also thought to myself, how am I going to deal with this identity crisis problem that I have been having all of my life? The bad thing is it was already to late to make up my mind. I was already sworn in.

The flight to California was a bumpy one. We hit a lot of turbulence. For me this was not good because this was my first time flying and I was getting motion sickness. I did find out that my motion sickness was worse on an airplane but I didn't barf (or loose my cookies) as I anticipated I would do. We finally arrived at Fort Ord, California about 7:30pm the evening of February 28, 1972.

Once there we were herded off of the bus as; "Cattle headed off to Slaughter." We met some Sergeants who were yelling at us to get us moving. The yelling was very similar to the type that the cowboys would use when they would round up cattle or horses into barns. It also bugged me because it was very similar to the yelling that I had been hearing all of my life from my dad at home. This is when I thought to myself, what did I get in too?

Some of us did not know how to handle this kind of garbage and racket. Is this what Boot Camp is going to be like? Are we going to experience discipline like this the whole time we are here? These questions were going to soon be answered.

By the time we got off of the bus it was time to go to the dinner hall (mess hall) to eat. We were told to hurry because it was still going to be a long night. There was a lot to be done before we could even head off to bed.

The processing in seemed like it took forever. We had to sign a bunch of forms and some of us had to get shots. When all of this was done there was some orientation. Finally we were assigned linen and our barracks. By the time we completed all of the processing it was about 2am the next morning. Wake up call was at 6:30am.

None of us received a whole lot of sleep that first night. I was too excited from the trip and everything. I had trouble falling asleep. By the time I closed my eyes it was time to wake up already. I was totally exhausted and wanted to just stay in bed. I did get up like the rest of the guys though.

We had to wolf down breakfast and be ready for more processing in less than an hour. From breakfast we went to get our haircuts, picked up our initial uniforms, followed by picking up our field gear. Between this issuing of equipment we also had more boring orientation classes and lunch. Our morning was filled.

The afternoon was already mapped out for us. It involved lunch, more orientation, and taking a battery of tests. These tests were to determine where our strengths and weaknesses are. They also helped the army to determine which area we are good in and which areas we could be of benefit to them. All of this made for another long day with very little sleep.

The next couple of days were no different. They also involved orientation and testing. By the end of the weekend we finally did get assigned to our training units.

My first weekend in the army I felt all alone. I really didn't know anyone. I also knew that I couldn't do what I was doing at home (my masturbating with cross-dressing). Not being able to do these for me was really very stressful. I'm not sure how I was going to handle it all of the way through Basic Training. I wasn't even sure I wanted too. Not with the yelling and screaming Sergeants. I thought that I had left all of that behind me with my dad. Why did I want more of it?

By the third week of training a group of the guys decided to try out the Enlisted Mans' Club located right there on the beach near San Francisco, California. Some of the guys invited me to go so I decided why not. I decided that there was nothing to loose.

I've always been one to take a risk or chances and was always open for new experiences. (Little did these guys know that I would rather have been there as a date in a dress instead of just one of the guys as a male). I also was so horny that I wanted to have sex one way or another. I think that this is why I got totally sloshed (drunk).

Once there we started off by having a few drinks. This way I could try to relax and forget the past few weeks at least for now. We then were able to strut our stuff and show off by competing against each other dancing.

Some of the guys were even cute when they danced. I even had a crush on one of the guys. I could not let him know that though because I would be out of the military for sure or I would have been beat up. Of course I was able to maintain even as drunk as I was.

We stayed there at the club until it closed. It was early in the morning when we headed back to our unit and many of us were staggering the whole way back. Once there at the barracks we kept the party going. Someone had beer and another had some pot. Finally someone turned up the tunes.

While partying I had the fantasy of giving everyone in the barracks a blow-job. Of course I knew that would never happen because I still was shy in this area. Our party didn't end until late in the morning.

Since we did not have to report for duty until Monday morning most of us slept in. I was one of those guys who got up early and headed to the mess hall for breakfast. I then planned to go into town again. I didn't want to go by myself though, so I convinced a couple of the guys to go with me. I'm such a sissy and a pussy at times when it comes to being alone in a new place, especially when I wanted to have a good time.

The bus took about 20 minutes to get from the base to Fisherman's Warf. We found out by the waiting that we could have walked the distance and made better time. I guess that's how one learns. Our plan was to walk back later in the day.

While at the Warf we did some rock climbing, walked on the beach, and did some swimming. (It would have been so much fun holding hands and being on the beach with just one man though). I started thinking to myself, "How romantic this could be.")

The area where we were had a bunch of no trespassing signs but we didn't care. Instead we just kept swimming and continued to play on the rocks. We also tripped on the waves that the Pacific Ocean was bringing in. For me this was a new scene having lived in the city all of my life.

After several hours we headed back for the Warf. When we reached it we decided to check out some of the food. Finally we chose a spot and I tried Octopus and fried Squid for the first time. Both of these were not that bad to eat. I in fact, enjoyed my meals.

By the time we were done with dinner it was getting late. I decided to head back to the unit. Some of the other guys were going to go back to the club and then to the barracks. I was too beat to go with them.

By the 4th week of Basic Training my asthma started to act up and I ended up in the hospital with a high fever. I knew that I didn't fit in with these guys because they did harder drugs while living in the barracks. I just wanted to be with the girls and being with guys was not for me.

When I got out of the hospital some of the guys ganged up on me and gave me a G. I. party, which was similar to those pink belly episodes we had in the eighth grade. The brushes were rougher and floor soaps added which caused my body to sting a lot. When all of this happened I really started to hate my training and said to myself, "Why are you here?" At the time I could not answer my own question. I just knew that I wanted to get out of this forsaken hellhole.

On the weekend of the 5th week a bunch of us headed to town. We were smart this time and got an early start. This way we could see the city and stay out all night if we wanted to. Too me the whole thing sounded like a blast.

By Saturday afternoon we found out that there was going to be a concert right there in the park. I thought that this would be a great opportunity to score. One of the guys wanted to score some pot because he was running low. Another wanted some acid and speed. I just went along for the fun of it and because this was a new experience for me.

We were right, the park was the place to be. Drugs and pot were right there in the open. People would walk right up to you and ask you to buy from them. The music wasn't too bad either. Neither were the women in their skimpy summer outfits. (In fact I envied some of them because I wished I were doing the same in a sundress.)

We stayed at the park for about 4 different bands. I was getting bored so I decided to head back to the base. I was so loaded that I crashed early that night without having anything to eat at the mess hall.

On Sunday we hit Salinas and Carmel early. Before noon I was wiped out from smoking pot. I also had a serious case of the munchies so I bought some food from one of the street venders. I kept eating all day long. Later we went to someone's house and continued to party. While there we smoked some more pot. I was getting totally wasted to the point of almost passing out. We then went for a ride in a Volkswagen Beetle. I was to sit in the back.

As we were riding I started to become violently sick from the crampness being in the back of a VW, and the motion of the car. It was as if I were poisoned or something. (These were the same feelings I had when I drank that day I barfed in the shoe store or when I would get severe motion sickness).

I didn't like these feelings at all so I asked to get out of the car. The car pulled over and the guys just left me off in the middle of nowhere. I had no idea where I was and it was already getting late so I decided to start hitchhike back to the base. Because I had no clue about where I was and was totally lost with being high, I actually hitched in the wrong direction.

My first ride took me about 20 miles in the wrong direction. I didn't realize this until I started to come down some from my high. I also asked for directions. Once I figured out what happened I headed back in the right direction. My next ride took me back to the Warf. From there I decided to hoof it in the rest of the way. The trip back took me hours because I must have walked at least 10 miles and I was still coming down off of the pot and booze. I reached the unit by 8:30pm.

When I made it back, I told the Sergeant on duty what happened to me. I mainly did this because I was pissed at the guys for dumping me in the middle of nowhere. I also ratted on the other guys about the drugs. Right after that the unit was called out for a shake down. None of them knew I squealed because I was at dinner when the shake down took place. They suspected that I was the rat though.

I was lucky that the dining room was still open because I started to get another case of the munchies. I ended up eating quite a bit while I was there. When I was done I headed back to the barracks and went straight for my bunk. I later found out that the next day I was going to be marching to the field and to the rifle range.

The field march was to be about 5 miles long. I was in terrible shape because of the booze, a hang over, and the pot from the night before. I also was starting to get very sick again. I was so sick that I was very weak and was hospitalized with Asthmatic Bronchitis.

At this point I thought about getting out of the army on a medical discharge. I was told that you had to have at least 120 days in before getting all of the benefits that the military had to offer. I decided that I would discuss my intentions with the Company Commander once I got out of the hospital.

I stayed in the hospital for about 2 weeks. I thought that if I miss 2-weeks I would have to take Basic Training over again.

Even though I was sick the hospital attendants put me to work doing light duty. I hated those very demeanial jobs. The time that I spent in the hospital allowed time for the trouble I caused by squealing on my peers to die down. It also gave me some time to think and plan what I was going to do once I was released.

When I returned back to the unit I headed immediately to the Charge of Quarter's (CQ) office. I told the Sergeant on duty that I wanted to talk to the commander in the morning. He said that he would pass the message on. I then headed for the mess hall for some chow and then straight to bed. Believe it or not I was glad to be back to a familiar place even though my building had been changed.

On Monday morning of the 6th week of training we had a march to the rifle range again. Before leaving for the range I talked with the First Sergeant and the Company Commander about getting out on a Medical Discharge because of my Asthma. The First Sergeant stated that he has been in for over 15 years and that he also has asthma. They both convinced me to stay in. I then told the commander that I hated guns and was afraid of them. The Company Commander stated that he would show me on the range that there was nothing to be afraid of.

This time I made the march to the range without any problems even though I did feel like dropping out. Then Company Commander took an

M-16 automatic rifle and placed it on the bridge of his nose. From there he fired it. He then asked for me to join him on the range. He had me fire off a few rounds. From that point on I felt that I was going to finish Basic Training no matter what. I ended up becoming really gun ho.

While doing hand-to-hand combat with padded puggal sticks I broke someone's collarbone. I was then told that I didn't know my own strength and that I had a natural killer instinct. At the time was this what I really wanted to hear? Those words kept me motivated and helped me through the rest of my training.

After 9-weeks of training I found out that I finally made it through Basic Training without having to retake any of the weeks missed over. I wasn't at the bottom of the list either, which was a surprise to me because of my hospital stay.

I was glad that the training was all over. From Basic Training I was going to take some time off and then go to Fort Carson, Colorado for Advanced Individual Training (AIT). I was promised tanker training and then to become an engineer.

I did fly back to Milwaukee, Wisconsin for my 30-day leave. During that time my high school was having their prom and I invited Sue's sister Pam. She accepted immediately. I was glad because I always had a high school crush on her.

When I picked up Pam she was not quite ready. I had to wait for her to put on the final touches of her make up and her gown. I found from experience that I am terrible at waiting for some one. I think that the military had something to do with that.

I was a gentleman though and picked Pam up at the door with bouquet in hand. From her house we dropped by my parent's home and stepped in to say hi to everybody. Dad as usual was not there. Mom of course snapped off a few pictures. She even told us that we looked like a great looking couple. She was right. I also thought that we looked great together.

Both of us enjoyed the prom but we did not want to stay long. Instead we headed for the beach and parked. While there we spent hours talking and making out.

I was all over Pam, but she knew when to stop me. We drank some alcohol and I went after Pam again. I finally listened to her because I felt that I really liked her. I always had liked her even when I was going out and screwing her sister.

The next couple of days I spent hours talking with Pam. I wanted to be with her all of the time but she didn't want me. I even told her I wanted to have her come back with me to Colorado. I proposed marriage to her a couple of times. When she flat out refused I was crushed.

Before going back to Ft. Carson I decided to buy a new car. I ended up buying a 1972 Gremlin. At the time I thought that it was cool looking vehicle and fast. My mom helped me buy it by co-signing for me.

The day after buying this car I headed to the beach on the east side. I wanted to score some pot, speed, or acid. I did buy some blotter acid and dropped it immediately. When I did I started to get a quick buzz. What I experienced was not what I expected.

I started to experience many racing thoughts. I also remember that my body began to hurt all over. These feelings stayed with me all day and part of the night. After several hours of these hallucinations I thought I was going to die. It also was hard to stay quiet in my parent's home. The next morning I drove back to Colorado in my new car.

When I left for Ft. Carson I decided to really test this car out. I floored it on the freeway and made what would be a 48-hour trip in 15 hours. The car handled very well at speeds 80-110 mph. I also was lucky because I drove at night and there was less chance of being pulled over by cops.

Shortly after I arrived at Ft. Carson I was told to report in. I did that and was released the rest of the day so I headed for the chow hall. While there I met some guys and they asked me if I had a way to get into town. I told them I had my own wheels but wanted to eat something first.

After chow we hopped into my car and one of the guys lit up a joint. We smoked about 2-3 joints during the 8-mile trip to town. Once in town we went looking for girls. I was the one that got lucky but the girl I met just wanted to run a scam on me by using my car. Of course I didn't know that at the time until after she was already been doing it. I also was to loaded to care.

I rented a motel room and she never did show up until later that evening. I was so wiped out that I crashed hard for at least 8 hours. I must have needed the rest after my long trip with very little rest prior to arriving at Ft. Carson, Colorado and the pot.

The girl I met convinced me into letting her use my car for a few days. She had the thing for about a week until I could get it back from her. She said that she would call me every day but never did. That is when I woke up and realized I've been had.

Throughout this time I tried not to worry about her and the car. Instead I partied with the guys I met a week earlier. They ended up being assigned a new unit after about 2 weeks and I had 1 more week to go before I would be assigned to my unit.

During that last week before my transfer I met another person that liked to smoke pot with. He turned me on to a joint and I told him he could find some good weed near the park down town. He also thanked me for that piece of information by keeping me high until I was assigned my own new unit.

By the end of my first year of the army I met a girl who also had had her share of problems. She was in a detention home for multiple problems including sex. I worked with the detention home and the state to get her out because I at the time thought that I was totally in love with her. I figured since I couldn't have Pam why not her. Finally I got her released to my custody in September of 1972. During this process I also kept getting into trouble but I tried not to let anyone know. Not even my folks.

Married To Young (Strike 1)
November 1972

Shortly after she was released we finally were able to have sex together. One thing I found out, Bambi loved to have sex and so did I especially when we were loaded. Her dad had given me consent to marry his daughter so in late September or early October we were married. Her dad gave his daughter away to me in front of the courthouse where the judge married us.

I had made a lot of friends in the apartment complex we lived in. Some of these friends were people I had been partying with in the past. Others just were excited about having and knowing young newlyweds who were in the military. They kept us high for about a week after we were married.

One day when I was off from work (by playing sick because I was to loaded to move), Bambi ran into that girl Jennie who used me in the past. Jennie was pregnant and Bambi said she had made friends with her. This blew me away because I thought that the girl was a real bitch. They both played a game on me and Jennie pulled out her gun, which was a .45 cal. Semi-automatic pistol. She played like she was going to shoot me. Bambi did the same thing. This totally freaked me out. I curled up into a ball and just broke into uncontrollable tears. I thought Bambi really loved me but doing something like this caused me to have second thoughts.

Later I figured that there must be something going on other than being just friends. I also knew that this marriage was not going to last to long with this kind of junk going on. How was I going to let Bambi know what I felt? Little did Bambi realize I was really getting screwed up by all of the drugs and booze that I had been doing all of these years? This is when I had my first nervous breakdown right then and there. I denied it of course because I didn't want to get any better. I also was to strung out by the drugs.

In November of that same year I decided to go to Medical Corpsman School at Fort Sam Houston, Texas. At that time I sent my new bride Bambi Lee, to my folks until I could get a place and settled at the school. I did not inform them of any of the other stuff that had been happening. I figured that they would figure all of that out for themselves and that they would let me know what was going on.

My folks informed me that Bambi was sleeping around with everyone in town. I figured that this was a story my dad made up because he and mom didn't like Bambi and because she would not sleep with him. My mom went along with his story under duress. They both thought that I should get her to Texas with me as soon as I could. Of course being a good obedient son I did as they asked even though I thought that they were exaggerating. This is why after about a month with my folks Bambi joined me in Texas.

During December of that same year, I decided that it was time to come out of the closet again. I started dressing in some of my new wife's' clothing. I bought a long hair wig at a yard sale, completely shaved off my mustache, and used her makeup. When she was out I would prance around the house in her long white see through nighty. It made me feel good to just be this way again. Of course I thought all of this was hidden.

Until this point I had never told Bambi that I had this problem with cross-dressing, but I knew in time that she would catch me sooner or later. That day did come.

One day I had on a white nightgown, the long hair wig and had made up my face. I even shaved off my mustache again in order to look and feel the part. I thought that would be okay to relax like this looking fully looking like a woman since Bambi was not at home and since I had the day off. I thought that Bambi would not be home for sometime. She surprised me and came home unexpectedly.

When she caught me I quickly started stripping off everything and tried to make up a crazy story, but could not come up with anything convincing not even to me. I ended up taking a risk by finally telling her the whole truth. Her response was that I had lied to her and that she could never trust me again. She also did something else that I never expected. She dressed in my army fatigues and went out in public that way. This was in a sense being dressed in male drag. That was something I didn't have the nerve to do even after cross-dressing all of these years. She figured if I could be a woman at home that she could be a guy in public. She played the part to the hilt even though to me she looked ridiculous. (I envied the guts it took to do what she was doing).

Near the end of December we finally met our neighbors. They were into Satanism. I had heard of Satanism but never really studied it in depth. Due to my curiosity I decided to check them out and tried to find out more about this cult. What I found out is that Satanism was pretty much like the opposite of Catholicism. Instead of believing in God, Christ, and the Trinity, they believed in Satan who was one of the fallen angels.

When I researched the subject by reading, and heard all of this I still wasn't sure about which way to go with my life. I was already screwed up from my drugs and alcohol and have been lost for a very long time at this point. Religion and a relationship with Jesus right now had been out of my life for a long time. I also was confused about who I was and which way I was going.

The guy stated he was a practicing Satanic Priest and had been one for quite some time. Either way I didn't care because I just wanted the drugs he had to offer. Eventually in time I even started to believe what they believed. Being an artist I even started to draw pentagons and satanic images, and started even to chant. The drugs made it all fall into place even easier.

Around the first of January 1973 our new friends got together with us for the New Year. We all decided to have a potluck drug party. We smoked some pot and did some pills. Then we decided to try the swinger or wife-swapping thing. This meant swapping wives or girlfriends and husbands. I figured why not, my marriage is on the rocks anyway. What did I have to loose? If everything ends now, so be it.

I did go through with the swapping of partners and Bambi started to but could not go through with it. This just meant more coal in the fire within our relationship. I knew that with the way that things were going that everything was not going to last too much longer with our marriage. I also knew that I was going to be divorced fairly early in this marriage.

After completing the medical training course we went back to Ft.

Carson, Colorado and I worked out of the hospital as an ambulance driver. A job like this was something I always wanted to do. I was pumped up for it.

While there I had a long ambulance run in upper Colorado. It was to pick up someone and head back home to Ft. Carson. I was supposed to go straight there and back. I figured that since this was a change in place I could take Bambi with me.

I picked her up from our trailer in Colorado Springs, Colorado and we were off and running. I took a detour to Bolder, Colorado to visit some of her old friends there first. After having an accident we were finally headed to pick up the patient. Late that night we finally did get there.

On the way home it started to snow heavily. I felt the ambulance swerve a lot by the wind. The road was also getting to slick for me to go on. The patient was not doing well so I pulled into Fitzsimons Hospital in Denver, Colorado. The patient did stabilize but we were left there with no money so I contacted the Red Cross and they set us up for a couple of days.

Eventually when I got back to Ft Carson I was in a lot of trouble. I ended up loosing my rank, being fined, being put on extra duty, and restricted to the barracks. Of course I didn't follow the restriction part because I still was a rebel. I also knew I couldn't trust Bambi anymore with anything in my life. Yes, I was paranoid, but I feel for just reasons.

By the July of this same year I went to another course at Ft. Sam. This time I thought I was going to become a Psyche Tech. I took Bambi with me this time. This was after being in a bunch of trouble and being busted down a rank at Ft. Carson.

While at Ft. Sam Houston, Texas, Bambi was very sick and had lost a lot of weight. She was pregnant with our first child at the time and was having episodes of false labor.

We were going to the hospital almost every other day or night. This was a lot of wasted hours and additional stress on me. I could not concentrate on my courses. After about 2 weeks into the program I was failing. By the 6th week I finally did fail out of this course and was shipped back to Ft. Carson, Colorado.

I then I sent Bambi back to her mom's to have the baby. I couldn't handle the stress and games any more. On the 10th of August of 1973 we finally did have a healthy baby girl.

When Tammy Lynn was born I was totally loaded on acid and speed. Bambi knew that I was stoned when she called me and she threatened me with the probability of not seeing my child if I didn't stop using my drugs. Shortly after the birth I was to report to Ft. Riley, Kansas for more training with a new company.

I made the trip to Ft. Riley loaded on pot, acid, and speed, and driving an old 1959 pickup truck. All of the guys I use to party with got me loaded for the road. I didn't even leave until early evening.

The truck that I drove during the trip kept overheating and finally totally broke down about 20 miles from the base. Of course this happened after picking up hitch-hikers and my falling off of the truck. The final breakdown happened in Wichita, Kansas. When the truck broke down I left it there and decided to hitchhike the rest of the way.

While doing so, I was offered the opportunity to spend the weekend in St. Louis. I figured why not, I have a couple of days off before I had to report in. I did spend the weekend in St. Louis and partied the whole time.

A good part of the time in St. Louis, Missouri I remained crashed out hard since I had been coming down off a long freeway high. I also thought that by being in St. Louis I might find my brother Tom who had been absent without leave (AWOL) from the army. I never did find him. I left St. Louis that Sunday late morning.

The first ride got me to Kansas City, Kansas. The guy was what I thought at the time weird. He showed me porn sex books and I sort of shined him on. He then pulled out his cock and wanted me to pull out mine. The incident was like a flash back into my childhood. I was not in the mood for his antics and still wiped out so I just asked the guy to drop me off at the nearest stop.

The next ride took me to Ft. Leavenworth, Kansas. He started me off by smoking a joint. We then had some straight whiskey. I was back into my buzz that I had that previous morning. By the time I hit Ft. Riley, Kansas I was totally buzzed and had a serious case of the munchies.

About 2 months after I arrived at Ft. Riley I did decide to clean up my act by getting completely off of the booze and drugs but only after I had realized all of trouble that I had been in even before I arrived there on the base. I knew that if I kept going the direction I was going that I would be either in prison or dead. I checked myself into a drug rehab program.

About 2-months after I arrived at Ft. Riley I found out that I was going shipped off to Germany for a training program called Reforger. Before going to Germany for this exercise I brought Bambi and the baby to join me there in Kansas. I warned her that I was only going to be gone about a month or so. I also gave her access to whomever she needed to be in contact with while I was gone that could get assistance if needed. She accepted that.

While I was away Bambi had messed up something fierce. She had the baby taken away from her because of child abuse. One of my neighbors had turned her in and got the base hospital involved. The problem was very serious and I ended up coming back stateside about a couple of weeks earlier than the rest of the troops.

When I did finally arrive back at Ft. Riley, I went to the hospital to see my baby, then to an attorney and court. I won the case hands down but was put on probation for something my wife had done. This had me upset and even a very pissed. I was about ready to kill Bambi.

I let her know how I was feeling and we never did do very well after that while I was still stationed in Kansas.

Bambi would always be sleeping around on me and kept stating that she was being raped. I of course was such a chump that most of the time I always believed her. Eventually I stopped believing her and we just argued continuously.

I went on a leave late in 1974 before being transferred back to Ft. Carson. We headed to California to visit Bambi's mom's home and went to see the rest of her family. We also wanted to show off our new baby. I told Bambi that I didn't want to let her family know anything about all of the problems that we have been having these past few years and while I was stationed at Ft. Riley.

While in California we did not let on totally about any of our marital problems. This was true at least until I completely screwed up. I thought initially for now it would be best to try to work out our problems and differences. I also was stupid and played my dumb ass male chauvinist games again. This time I slept with and had intercourse with Bambi's younger cousin. By doing so this made our welcome and visit with Bambi's family shorter than anticipated. We left California a few days after the incident but on shaky ground. I knew because of this episode that Bambi and I would not be together within a year from this point on.

She did not want to come back to Colorado with me but was forced to by her mom to go with me. In hindsight we both realized that this decision was a big mistake. I also knew that I didn't love her any more even though at first I thought I did. We spent the rest of 1974 at Ft. Carson, Colorado.

While at Ft. Carson I made my military ranks very fast once I kept my act straight. We survived the probation of the previous year that we were given from the state of Kansas. I was still cautious though because I could not trust Bambi alone with our daughter and with other men.

In June 1975 I was to head for Germany. I had just made the rank of Sergeant and completed my Expert Field Medical Badge (EFMB). Bambi was sleeping around again and causing me trouble. I ended up flunking out of the NCO Academy because of all of these problems. I also was still very immature but I was fortunate because the post General went to bat for me.

After spending about a week with my folks I sent Bambi back home to her mom's again until I could send for her once settled in Germany. I told her that with all that had been happening throughout all of our marriage, that she could divorce me and I would not contest it. This tour in Germany was for a regular 3-years and I wanted to make the best of it while I could.

While in Germany I hit the booze and pot again. Besides the booze and pot I tried to make it with some of the girls in the whore houses in Frankfurt. I didn't care if I was married or not. I even paid for sex at one of these Whore Houses.

Bambi joined me in Germany after about 6 months. Once she arrived in Germany, she seemed colder to me than usual. Later I found out that she did not want to come join me and that her mom convinced her to come again. Apparently while at her mom's she had been having an affair with someone in California that she liked a lot. She had also been doing some serious partying of her own. Later I found out from her mom that she was going to divorce me. I didn't know what had been going on so I sent for her and the baby.

About three months with me in Germany Bambi decided that that she wanted to divorce me and that would be the end of it. Her timing was very crappy because she told me all of this on my 23rd Birthday. When this happened I was in a panic and tried to do all that I could to put it all back together. Again I broke down into uncontrollable tears (another nervous breakdown). She convinced my friends that I was the one who was wrong and that she was not the problem. The marriage lasted only another couple of months.

As the marriage ended I just about killed Bambi with my own hands. She had been very lazy while watching our little one. Tammy Lynn had cut herself and destroyed the wall of one of the rooms in our off base apartments.

While we lived in the military quarters Tammy pulled off her diapers, and had started to learn to climb. This time she climbed to the top of the refrigerator and knocked over a whole bag of flower. Bambi was so lazy that she didn't even bother to clean up the mess. Bambi also would leave her used tampons and cigarettes lying around on the floor. All of this happened again while I was in the field on maneuvers.

The mess with the dirty diapers, tampons, etc., lit the fuse that made me blow my top (temper).

Bambi was repeating the pattern of abuse that she had done 2 years prior. I did not want everything to start all over again since now I have come so far with cleaning up my act. I decided that she wasn't going to destroy everything that I worked so hard to rebuild.

I took Bambi with my hands and started to strangle her around the throat right in front of everyone at he enlisted mans USO Club in Aschafenburg, Germany. Someone yelled at me to stop and I eventually did. After I did, I ran out of the club and went back to the quarters. I was a nervous wreck again (my 3rd breakdown). Several hours later I was locked up by the MP's for making a public scene, and my assault on Bambi.

Shortly after the whole incident happened, my Commanding Officer came down to bail me out. I showed him what had happened and when he saw the mess he said, "You should have just thrown her out of the window, I know that I would have done." Until this day I think that he was right.

I ended up being restricted to the barracks for the next 2 weeks for the incident. While I was there Bambi started sleeping around again. She and I decided to separate while in Germany. We felt that it would be best especially since I almost did kill her in front of everybody.

Once I was off of restriction, I went to the JAG Office and had divorce papers made up. I also made sure that Tammy Lynn was taken out of the picture by shipping her home to be with my parents. This was a hassle because I had to get her own special passport. That meant I had to make a trip to Heidelberg, Germany.

I decided that the trip would be worth it in the long run so I went for it. I took Tammy with me and we made the drive in about 6-hours. Since we were early we enjoyed one of the parks and some of the castles in this city. Finally got Tammy shipped home 15 days after all of the divorce stuff started.

While at home I asked my mom to help me get the divorce started in Milwaukee, Wisconsin using the papers I had JAG make up. I also told her I was going to get started on getting out of the military early so I could raise Tammy by myself.

Once I got back in Germany, Bambi decided that she was going to move in with any guy she wanted. At first she did not want to go back home to the states. She lived with several guys for several months. Finally after seeing that it wasn't easy living in Germany she did decide to leave. It took 2 tries to get her sent home. During the time that she was in Germany she was making things look bad for me by getting in trouble.

When Bambi was home and out of the picture I decided to do some of my own partying again. I went back to the booze and smoking pot. I lived on base because I knew that it was easier to stay loaded there. I also befriended one of the dishwashers from the base. All that she wanted to do was to have sex. She even wanted to do it in public for the whole world to see.

When I was high I would go with the flow but not in the middle of the beach near the Rhine River and Aschafenburg Castle. Having sex like this was a little too much for me. I couldn't act like a dog at times and just be as open as this girl was. I was getting hung up on this girl but she did eventually dump me because I didn't follow her plans.

At one point I went out with one of the local bar maids. She convinced me to drive her up to Northern Germany to visit her family. This was an interesting experience for me and I did enjoy it.

German families are not much different from Americans. Her family was very accepting and sociable. I was totally accepted even with my gay tendencies.

By this time I was getting fed up with the military. I decided that I should try to get out of the army but with an Honorable Discharge. As I had already said I had my mom help me with some of the paperwork needed to get out. This meant statements from ministers, neighbors and family. I also returned to my masturbating and stayed naked in my room when I was there. I was going for a Hardship Discharge, which was also an Honorable one.

Receiving the discharge would be very easy because of what had just happened with my violent scene, the parting, the sex in public and my Severe Depression from remaining separated from my daughter.

About a month prior to being discharged I had an appointment to be seen by a Psyche Doctor in Frankfurt. The psychiatrist saw that there were definite emotional problems going on with me and agreed that I should be discharged.

The whole process of getting out took about 3 months once I got the paperwork going. It was this quick because I walked what paperwork I could through personally. If I went through channels the process would have taken a lot longer.

While living in the barracks I would try to stay to myself a lot. I would party with the guys at first and then would head for my room. One of the guys always wanted to barrow money to gamble. When he asked me I always had some. After about 3-4 times of loaning him what he needed, I started to charge him 150% interest. I mainly did this to teach him a lesson. He would always agree to this amount.

About a month prior to getting out of the military I went on some field maneuvers and was put in charge after making friends with one of the First Sergeants. I was to relieve the person that always borrowed from me because he was not doing his job.

When I did so the First Sergeant was with me. This guy cursed me out in front of him and ended up showing me no respect when I relieved him from duty. I was going to let it slide but the First Sergeant wanted this guy busted down a couple of notches. This was bad because this individual had been the military over 11 years already. He was busted down 2 ranks without a statement from me. He also never borrowed money from me again.

While in my room I would always play my music loud and lye in my bed naked. I did this because I was so horny that all I wanted to do was masturbate. I would masturbate for hours at a time and several times a day. When I did this I would have the fantasy that I was a woman with a man just fucking the hell out of me. I even got busted doing this when I had my music to loud one night.

Before getting out of the military I decided to check out some of the local "Off Limits" bars. These are the ones that had nude dancers and were usually X-to-XXX rated. I didn't mess around with just beer at this point. I went for Conjac and Coke.

One night when I ordered my first drink I guzzled it right down. The bar owner saw me do this so he decided that he was going to, "Pull the Wool Over on Me," by giving me 7/8 of Conjac and 1/8 coke. He didn't think I saw what he did or could handle it being a GI. At that time I was a smart ass and guzzled it just like the first drink. When I did this the owner gave me my drinks on the house for the rest of the night. (Later I found out he was gay and wanted me to be totally drunk so that he could have his way with me for sex). Until this day I should have taken him up on his offer. Instead I held my wits about me and didn't let that happen. At least not yet even though I wanted it and knew at this point I was bisexual.

I finally got out of the military by the end of June of 1976. Boy was I happy when this happened. The problem was though I didn't know what to do so I lived with mom and dad for a couple of months. This was a disastrous decision on my part. I felt out of place and didn't want to grow up. I did try it though for all that it was worth.

You are out of the Army, Now what?
-1976

As I said I finally got out of the military by the end of June 1976. Boy was I happy when this all happened. The problem was I didn't know what to do so I lived with mom and dad for a couple of months. I was not use to this and felt completely out of place. My dad thought that I didn't want to grow up. He also had not changed with his abuse toward mom and this drove me crazy.

At first I did try to live at home for a bit and go back to school. I figured I would go for my Nursing Degree at the University of Wisconsin. Of course like everything else I tried this was on the spur of the moment and not completely thought through. I also did not think about Tammy. She was my responsibility now and I had to accept it. I did attend classes for about 2 weeks and found out I could not handle both. Shortly after dropping out of college I moved out of my parents' home. When this happened I ended up going on welfare.

Tammy became a real burden on me. I saw this because I was having a real problem raising her when I was living in a 1-room apartment and could barely get by, especially since I did not have a job yet. I also knew that I wasn't being fair to Tammy because I was still so immature. During this time I even wanted to start a new relationship with someone male or female and having a child already made that a lot more difficult to do.

While on welfare, I did meet a girl. I met her through one of my younger brothers who had dated her before.

She had the nickname of "Murph." She told me that she received this name because of her size and because people thought that she looked like one of the cartoon Smurf characters.

I tried to be with her as much as I could. This was very hard having a little one to care for. I was able to make arrangements with one of my other brothers when I wanted to be alone with her. The only thing is this would only be temporary.

By Christmas of 1976 my folks decided to pack up and move to Florida for good. This meant that I had no resources to fall back on if I would have any problems in the future with Tammy Lynn. When this happened I had to do things like raising Tammy (my daughter) completely by myself. This was something that I was not ready for, at least not now. I was too immature, messed up, and selfish. This is why I decided to let Tammy go with my parents and concentrate on my own career.

Me a Shoe Salesman and a Manager?
-December 1976

By December of 1976 I landed a job as a shoe salesman. The manager saw that I had ability to sell and by the end of 2 weeks I was in training to become the Assistant Manager. I still had not set up baby-sitting for Tammy. All I had was my brother and his family. The reality is all I wanted to do was get back to the partying as I had already started to do in Germany. With Tammy out of the picture that is what I did. I also put in a lot of hours on the job.

About 3 months after Tammy left with my folks to Florida my dad sent her back to me. This is when I asked my brother Tom to help me out which he was only able to do for about a month or so.

Once these arrangements were made I felt that I might be able to handle raising Tammy and work. Boy was I dead wrong. Then the unexpected happened. Tom could not help any more and I could not manage caring for Tammy by myself. Now I had to raise Tammy again and also work. I could not handle the stress of this added responsibility.

I truly tried to raise her and even did something stupid leaving her asleep in the cold car. I almost was arrested for this blunder and just about lost Tammy for good. Eventually I didn't know what to do with her while I was at work. I ended up dumping her with my brother Tom and his family.

On my days off I did try to spend quality time with her by entertaining her and taking her to new places and talking with her. I also started abusing Tammy physically and emotionally which is what her real mom had done to her the first five years of her life. By the time that I realized that I was doing this I felt very guilty. These feelings were only short lived. Eventually I couldn't take it anymore.

For her safety I decided to place Tammy with the state of Wisconsin.

I figured that since I couldn't raise her, and my folks didn't want her, that what I did was the only thing I could do. This is when I made one of the hardest decisions I ever made in my life.

I gave Tammy up to Child Protective Services (CPS) for her welfare. In hindsight this again was a very big mistake. It really showed the selfish side of me, but it happened and I cannot change what I did.

Once Tammy was out of the picture, I felt that I could basically do anything that I wanted to do without any responsibilities. This even meant partying again as I had done in the past since all I had to only take care of was me. The partying included getting involved in heterosexual and homosexual relationships. Doing this was not unusual because of my past. Until this point I was not sure about which direction I was going to take.

Too many things were happening very fast and I was not even sure I could handle all of it especially emotionally. I had given up the one love of my life, my daughter, because I was becoming just like her mother. I was not even sure why I even acted this way.

I was working hard and doing very well selling woman's shoes. In fact, I was the only assistant manager ready to move up into managing my own store in less than 6 months. I also was the best salesman in the district and everyone new it. Besides working in retail I started working for the Wisconsin National Guard.

While working for the guard I was activated for about 2 weeks. Our unit was to manage the adolescent detention camp. I did well during this assignment and even received a promotion. I also hooked up with one of the older kids who moved in with me shortly after he had bee released. Shortly after all of this happened I entered into a gay relationship.

This gay relationship was the first time in my life that someone appeared to care for me for who I am (so it seemed). The incident also reminded me of the relationship I had when I was younger. The difference is I was more experienced and capable of sharing more passion and emotion when going down on this guy. When we finished having sex he wanted me to quit my job and move in with him. I declined but later I regretted this decision.

In sales I could sell multiple pairs of shoes with accessories even better than the manager who trained me. I proved this during the Easter sale. I was selling 2 pairs to every 1 pair of shoes he sold. It was like we were competing against each other and I had become very good at it. I also was very creative and had a knack for remembering long numbers. This ability helped me picture and remember various shoe stock locations.

When all of this compositeness was going on, the present District Manager was there in the store. He just watched us compete against each other and was very impressed by what he saw. Later he even informed my manager that he wanted me to run his home store in Cudahay, Wisconsin within the next few weeks. Boy did this give a boost to my ego. I received that bit of news during the next week and was being trained up on doing the inventory and the books. Those few weeks came very quickly.

I was headed for my first assignment as a fill in manager. We did the inventory and then the store was all mine for the next month. I was very hard boring work though and I did put in a lot of hours each day and week. Those hours did not include the hour drive to and from work.

Managing a store for the first time was a challenge. I found out that I had a lot to learn and I did make quite a few mistakes. My biggest weakness was in the area of bringing the customers into the store. For me I did not see this as a problem because I felt that I already learned a lot from my manager and had some of my own ideas about sales. He also had given me some unusual ideas for displaying shoes inside the window and the store. The bad part about all of this is that I later found out I was wrong a good part of the time.

I was trying to equally match the weekly sales of the previous year. This was a tough task because there were not as many clients coming into the store as the previous year. That is why the store was loosing money. All I could do was do my best and hope I did as well.

Since there were not many employees assigned to the store I was doing most of the stocking myself. The display windows were very small so I really did not have much to work with. This meant that I had to make the inside of the store pleasing to the eye, which was a very tough job since the store was so small and old. I did survive the month and headed back to the original store I had been training at.

Once back working at my home store, I started to train other sales people and another assistant manager. I would work very closely with these people and tried to train them the way I was trained. This meant also teaching them how to stock shoes on the shelves in the back according to style and number. There was some resistance at first but when I explained to them that by stocking the items you get an idea on where the items are when you are making a sale. After I explained all of this everyone just jumped in and there was no more friction.

Shortly after I returned to the home store I received a report about how I did during that month I managed the District Managers store. Apparently he felt that I did do quite well. Oh, I did not do a perfect job but I did well enough to be considered for more management training. Several weeks later I received that opportunity. I was headed for St. Paul, Minnesota.

The drive to St. Paul was about 6-8 hours and I drove straight through the night to get there. I arrived about 9:00am and reported in at the store. The new District Manager I was to work under was there to meet me and he suggested that I get cleaned up and report back to the store in a couple of hours. I did as he said.

When I reported in the second time we started off by doing an inventory of the store items. This meant going through every item in the store by using a checklist. Our goal was to make sure everything balanced out before the old manager could leave. The inventory took us about 2 days and then the store was mine to manage.

This store was significantly bigger than the last one I managed but it still had small windows so I had a problem with displaying the shoes in these windows. What was working for the store is it was in one of the largest malls in the area. Also there were a lot of huge floor displays, which I was not used too. I knew that I could work with the new concept but it would be tough one to learn especially since now I was working under an older and different District Manager.

Shortly after I started to run the store some of the sales people and an assistant manager quit. This left me with one other person to run the store with me. When this happened I let the new District Manager know about this problem right away.

It took him some time to respond to the problem. Once he did respond he stayed to run the store with me until I could hire a new crew.

Hiring a crew took me a couple of weeks. I worked with the new crew for a few weeks. I knew that there was no way that I would be able to have them completely trained by the time I was to head back home in 2 more weeks. All I could do was do the best I could and hope for the best. Again the time managing this new store did go by very fast.

I went back to my home store and explained to my manager that I did not like what had happened. I told him I did not really have the training or the support I needed from this new District Manager. He tried to listen but I deep down I think that he did not really care. He to thought I did well.

A couple of weeks later I went back to St. Paul. This time everything ran a lot smoother. I was there for another month. I also knew that this time I probably would be considered for running my own store soon. When that month was over I went back to my home store and about a month later I found out I was being assigned my own store in Springfield, Illinois. I had to report there within 2 days. This meant packing up everything and making a major move for me. I was able to make this all happen and again reported after making a long drive during the start of winter.

The District Manager I had back in St. Paul was going to be managing over me again here. I felt skeptical about this because I felt he was of no support before and I really didn't like him. What made him think he would be any help now?

I came back the following day and we started doing another major inventory. This time the inventory took us about 3 days. It took this long because we had to go over everything more than once. The reason is the manager I was replacing had apparently been stealing from the store. This is why he was being replaced.

By the time that the inventory was completed we did find a significant shortage. The previous manager had to make up that difference prior to me taking over the store. This way I would be receiving a store with a fresh start and I could either make it productive or allow it to close.

Again shortly after I started to run my own store the assistant manager quit. This time the incident happened when the District Manager was still with me in the store so he stuck around to see how I would handle everything.

I was by myself only a couple of days. I hired a high school kid part-time. He learned how to sell very quickly so the District Manager left. A week later I hired another individual as an assistant manager. By doing so, I could go out into the mall and look at the various displays and even recruit other salesman.

The mall in Springfield was as huge as the one in St. Paul. It also was the only one in the area which gave it a potential for being successful. There were a lot of shoe stores there so I knew I would have a lot of competition. I also knew that because the shoes my store were specialized specifically for women I might have an advantage.

When I went into a store I talked to some of the salesman and managers. I even introduced myself as the new manager of Malings shoes. I let everyone know that if it did not work out where they were working that I would consider hiring and training them in my store.

About 2 weeks after I hired my assistant manager trainee he decided that he wanted a raise. I told him that I could not do that right away because he had not been working for me long enough. I also let him know that he could make the raise happen if he put in more hours and made a lot of sales. He said he would try. A couple more weeks went by and this assistant asked for a raise again. When I informed him that he couldn't have one he decided to quit.

About 2 days later I had a black salesman apply for the vacant assistant manager position. I hired him right on the spot and immediately started training him. He already could sell because he came from one of my competitors. All I had to do was to teach him the stock and paperwork.

Less than a week went by and I was able to hire a couple more black sales people. Both were friends of the new assistant manager. They seemed to get along well and now I felt I had a full new crew. I worked with them a couple of weeks until I felt that I could leave them alone to run the store.

During this time I started to party again. I even came to work one night totally wasted and watched my new crew work. They all knew I was wasted so they ignored me for a while.

I hung around a while and waited for the store to close. I then did the books and went out with everyone to one of the local clubs where they had a live band. We partied until early morning. I even got lucky and met a college girl who ended up staying the whole night with me.

By this time I had to dress up the display windows. I had my oldest employee the high school kids help me. He would hand me the shoes and accessories as I placed them in creative ways in the window display.

While I was dressing the window my District Manager dropped in on me for a surprise visit. He looked at my windows and did not like what he saw. He also checked out my black crew and wanted me to get rid of all of them right away.

I informed him that I would keep my crew because for me they were working well together. Little did I know that they would not last anyway. He then became upset with me and wanted to go over my window displays with me.

He said that I could not display my items the way I was doing. He even asked me to redo the displays which I was hesitant to do. This is when I asked him for some suggestions or that if he thought that he could do these displays better. He did not give me any suggestion and ignored the second part of my question.

I made some minor changes to the displays and left the rest. I figured that this was my first time doing displays in my own store and that I would learn from my own mistakes. I also felt that I needed to stand my own ground since this new store was like a second home to me.

Business in the shoe store did start to pick up but only by very little. My creativity in the windows helped only s slight bit. I think that this happened because I displayed items differently than my competitors. My creativity did show and this is an area where shined.

Now it was getting closer to the Christmas holiday. This meant that it was time to change out the window displays again and make them ready for the Thanksgiving and a Christmas sales.

I started working on the windows while my black crew was working in the store. This time it seemed like the dressing of the windows was taking a lot longer than usual. I had no help and started to feel all-alone again. Then out of the blue my black crew walked out on me and completely quit. Now I was truly alone running the store again. I tried to notify the District Manager and this time was never successful. He never did get back with me.

My display windows were not even done when this happened. Because I was stuck managing the floor completely by myself I closed and locked the windows and left them as they were. I did my best to keep the store open until my part-time school aged salesman came into work. After he did show up I was able to work on the window display again. By closing time I had completed about ¼ of the work needed to complete them. I knew I had a long way to go so I locked up the windows again and after closing the store started working on completing and transmitting my paperwork. All of this took me until about 10:00-11:00pm. By the time I was done I was so exhausted so I headed straight home and to bed.

The next morning I woke up late and ended up opening up the store late. This upset me because I usually am never late for anything. Being late this time actually got me in trouble but I didn't care anymore.

Shortly after opening up the store the first assistant manager I hired came back. He wanted to be rehired as my assistant again. Since I had no staff I hired him back at the same rate that was making before. Since he was trained already it gave me a chance to finish working on that window display.

Business was slow so I was able to finish the display with time to spare. It ended being this way for about a week so I started to get worried because sales were down. I thought to myself, what can I do to bring business up again? This is when I decided to check out the competition.

I did so with my new assistant and found that my displays were very radical from the others in the mall. I also was able to meet with other managers who were doing the same thing I was doing as far as sales and was invited to party with them. At that time I chose not to do so. I was just stressed out by what had happened to me these past couple of weeks. Having hindsight, I should have taken them up on getting high, but that is the past.

Immediately after Thanksgiving I decided to make some major adjustments to my display window. I started working on the window again but this time I was fed up with the way my District Manager was supporting me so the motivation that I had previously was not there. I also decided enough is enough so just before Christmas when my main salesperson came in I came out of the display window and threw him the keys telling him that he now is the new manager of the store. I also told him he should call the District Manager to let him know what happened and that I quit. I then headed out of the store never to return again.

Hit the Road Jack
-December 1977

As I was heading out of the parking lot of the Springfield, Illinois Mall I had no true clue about what I was going to do or where I was headed. All I knew is that I was leaving with my old assistant manager from the Malings shoe store for the road. I did drop by the apartment I was staying at and picked up most of my clothes prior to heading northwest. We headed out in 2 cars and really only enough cash to get about half way to California.

To me that didn't matter because I know I was away from all of the stress I had been experiencing while managing my own store. The bad part is if I had true support from my District Manager, I might have stayed to make the store work and make money.

Now one might think that I was this running away from my problems? You bet it was. Was this the right thing to do? Maybe during the time that everything happened it was, but in hindsight today I believe leaving as I did was completely wrong. I also know that when I left I was very immature and messed up on my alcohol and marijuana again and didn't care anymore.

As we were driving on the freeway I drove safely by staying close to the speed limit. I also had a CB-radio so I had an idea about where the hot spots that cops were hiding.

My traveling partner in the 1963 Chevrolet II drove like a maniac. He would speed and drive with his feet looking backwards. Eventually after some time he did get caught. When this happened I was able to pass him up without any problems. Even with these problems happening, we still continued on our trip.

Finally when we reached Colorado we started to run out of money. This is when we decided to sell one of our cars. Of course the one I was driving was the only one that would sell and I received less than $200.00 for it. I also sold my CB-radio separately, which brought our amount of cash to about $250.00. After these sale I then purchased a backpack and some good hiking shoes. Once I had all of these items I backed up the backpack full and loaded it up into the Chevrolet and we were back on our way. This time we decided to head for Canada. We drove the rest of the evening completely through and came to the Browning, Montana exit which was a direct drive into Canada.

At first we tried to cross the Canadian boarder legally. When we talked with the boarder guard he would not let us in because we were so low on money and only had one credit card between us. This threw us for a loop so we decided to see if we could find another way to cross the boarder illegally. This thought was a bomb because there was a lot 4-foot fencing around the boarder and waist high snow drifts that a car could not drive through. We found all of this out after driving all night.

By morning we decided to dump this car and walk over the boarder. Once over the boarder we decided the best way to travel to Calgary Alberta Canada was to hitchhike.

Finally we found a small town outside of the boarder. We pulled our last car into a high snow bank, grabbed our backpacks and started walking over the Canadian boarder.

What are you doing in Canada?
-December 1977

It seemed like we walked for hours because the snow was above our knees and both of us were cold and soaking wet. By the time we estimated that we traveled about 3-4 miles, we headed for the main road. After we hit the main road we realized that we did travel actually only 2 miles over the boarder. We were lucky because we received a ride about 30 minutes after we started to hitchhike. The ride that we received was in the back of a pickup truck and the individual giving us the ride was a full-blooded Indian. He took us to his house were we were able to get a meal and a roof over our head. All we had to do is to be honest with our host and his family.

This whole situation for me reminded me of those years that I studied Indians and folklore especially when I saw how these Indians lived and how the deer meat was curing on a tree in the back yard. I remember learning a lot from those books.

As I stated we had a warm meal and were able to have a roof over our head for the night. After eating I pulled up a couch and tried to sleep. I still was cold from our walk over the boarder and somewhat troublesome and excited because I never have done anything like this in my life before.

By the time I got to sleep on the floor it was about time to get up and back on the road again. It was like I never slept at all, but I did get a couple of hours rest. When we did get up our host gave us a ride to the main road again.

It seemed like it took hours before we received our first ride. I think we walked for about an hour or so and finally we received a ride that took us to the outskirts of Calgary, Alberta Canada. We arrived in Calgary in the early afternoon and not very much was open due to the Christmas and New Years holidays.

As we continued to walk my traveling partner informed me that he knew of a place that we might be able to stay. The thing is this place was clear across town. We would have to walk in the cold since we did not have any money. I let him know that I was game, but really deep down inside I would rather have taken a cab or something.

While we walked along the main streets I started to examine the stores. Calgary was an older town. Some of the buildings looked as they had been there for quite some time.

Finally we made it to our destination. It was a hostile (a place where true Canadians could receive financial aid, a meal, and a place to stay). All that we had to do was pretend that we were Canadian.

There are many of these hostiles throughout Canada. Anyway when we finally did arrive at our destination we found out that there was a huge line outside the front door.

By the time the line came to us the place was full and we were turned away. This was terrible because we didn't have a place to stay for the night. We did find out though that there was a bar close by that stayed open all night. They also had food and something to drink there. After finding this out we headed for that location.

Boy was the place crowded. There were a lot of street people like us there sitting in the chairs. Some of them had already fallen to sleep. There also was music, and woman to dance with. The unusual thing I found out though is that the men do not ask the woman to dance at these clubs.

The women ask the men. If you do things like asking the girls to dance the traditional way, then the Canadians know that you are not from Canada. We ended up spending the night at this location.

By morning I started to get hungry. There was a pawnshop close by but it did not open until about 10:00am. Here it was only 8:00am. What were we going to do for the two hour wait? We decided to head back to the hostile and see if we could get a room. This would kill time and we could deal with the pawnshop later.

This time we got there early enough and we were able to luck into having a place to stay for the night. After this happened we headed back to the pawnshop.

I ended up pawning a ring, a watch, and a silver bracelet. With the money I bought us a meal and still had enough for a bed at the Salvation Army center for a later time.

We were at the hostile a couple of days when my hitchhiking partner decided that he was going to ditch me. When this first happened I freaked out but after concentrating and pulling myself back together I decided that I would stay in Canada for about one more day and then hitchhike down to Orange County California. So now that I had a plan, I was not feeling to bad. The next couple of nights I did spend in the Salvation Army.

While I was there I found another individual that wanted to hitchhike south with me. He said that he lived in the southern part of Canada and invited me to join him since he knew I was going back to the United States anyway. We both left after my second day and headed for the main street of Calgary and the highway.

Our walk was a tough one but as soon as we reached the main highway we received our first ride. This ride took us directly to my new hitchhiking partner's hometown. From there we only had to walk a short distance to his house.

By the time we arrived at his home it was already late in the evening and was invited to spend the night and have a hot meal. I talked with him and his family for a bit, had a sandwich, and went right to sleep.

Early in the morning I got up and packed up my things for my long hall to California. As I was finally ready to leave my host gave me a sandwich for the road.

From this location it did not take me long to make it back to the Canadian and United States boarder. This time I pulled out my drivers' license and was able to walk over the boarder legally.

Back in the United States and Headed for California
-January 1978

Once back in the United States I don't know why, but I felt safe again. As I was walking from Browning, Montana I started to eat my sandwich. I waked and ate.

This was the most I have walked in a long time and I was getting tired easily. I wasn't getting a ride because it was very cold outside, and there was almost no traffic.

As evening started to come a highway patrolman drove by. He asked me where I was heading and where I came from. I was honest with him and told him I had just been to Canada and was heading for Orange County California.

He offered to allow me to stay in an open cell for the night. I told him I would help the cooks in the morning feed the prisoners if I could get a small meal for myself. He took me up on this offer.

Morning came quickly. I was up by about 5:00am and I did help the cooks out in the kitchen. Shortly after the prisoners ate, I received my meal, which was luke warm.

I wasn't going to complain though because at least I had a meal. I wolfed down this meal quickly and gathered my pack together making sure I had enough warm clothes on for my trip.

Shortly after I arrived back on the main highway, I received a ride immediately. This ride took me all of the way to Victorville, California. The trip took about 1 1/2 days.

During this ride I was able to catch a catnap. I think I would have slept more have a problem with motion sickness. This is a problem that has been with me all of my life and I have not been able to shake it.

We finally arrived in Victorville, California early in the morning. At the rest stop I offered to do work for a meal. The owner fed me for free.

Shortly after eating I was getting tired. In fact, because it was so early I decided to try to pull out my sleeping bag out and catch another nap in the near by rest stop. Doing so was an experience, but I did get about a 2-hour rest prior to getting back on the road to hitchhike again.

It took me about 30 minutes to get another ride but the ride took me all of the way to Orange, California. This is where my soon to be ex-mother-in-law lived.

I arrived at her place at about 9:00am. She was home and offered me a meal and informed me that I could not stay with her. I updated her about what was happening and ate the meal without any arguments. After eating I headed toward Harbor Boulevard, which was close to Disneyland.

I tried to hitchhike, but no one would pick me up so I ended up walking the whole way, which ended up being about 5-6 miles. Once there I started applying for different jobs. Before 6:00pm I did land a job at a western boot store. The manager said I could start the next day. This was great but I still did not have a place to stay so I ended up sleeping on the grounds in a mobile home park sleeping under a trailer for the night.

The next morning I started to work at my new position. The manager started me off by working by cleaning up the store. He also had me run to the local Dunk'n Donut Shop, which was less than a block away.

While we ate he asked me to give him some history about myself. I ended up being very brief and informed him that I left my last manager position because I did not have any support from the district manager. He then gave me an idea about what I would be doing and I listened intently.

After our talk and the food I went back to work and put in a full day. I was out by about 6:00pm, and again I still did not have a place to stay. I went to the mobile home park again and this time I found a vacant bus that I slept a few hours in. I then slept under a trailer as I did the previous night.

The next morning I cleaned up a bit in the restroom located in the trailer park before I went to work. This next day at work turned out exactly the same as the first day. I was able to start stocking shoes though, which made the day go by somewhat faster. By the end of my shift I was actually pretty tired. After work I headed for the trailer park again and my routine was the same all of the way through Saturday.

To my surprise I actually received my first check early so I grabbed a local newspaper and tried to find a place that supplied room and board. I was lucky because I found a place after only a couple of calls. This was great because now I would have a home base and finally have to stop sleeping in the street with the rain and the cold. I was also able to buy some clothes from the local goodwill that I could use for work.

I was off on Sunday and back to work that following Monday. This gave me the opportunity to learn the bus system and how to walk to work if I had too. I was able to familiarize myself with the shortest ways to work and I also started planning some other things for myself.

While in the boarding house I tried to interact with my peers and from what I had found out a bunch of them were a lot sicker than I was. I felt bad for the homeowner who was a nurse because she was the one caring for these 6-10 mentally ill men. I did learn later on from these men that this nurse mainly took advantage of them and that it all was about keeping their Social Security or SSI checks. Those checks paid for the mortgage and then some. I worked the whole next week as usual.

While at work my old manager from Malings Shoe's called the store. My boss talked with him and then I explained what I felt had happened and that I was very displeased with the way I was treated.

After the call I went back to work. This week went by very quickly and I received my second check. I paid for my room and bought a bicycle from one of the kids where I was living. I decided to do so I could save some money on transportation.

By the time I had been working in the store for about 2 months I was able to save enough money to buy a car. Around this same time I met Beverly who I ended up hooking up with.

She had a multiple personality disorder and was bipolar. She also was very childlike and I sort of felt sorry for her. We became friends very quickly and did go out a few times. This happened for another month or so before I decided I had to leave California to deal with the final part of my first divorce.

One night I just quit my job packed up my things in my car, we gathered up her things and just started to head out of Orange County

California. Prior to leaving Beverly tried to say goodbye to her folks and her dad did not want anything to do with her so we just left.

Two on the Road Again.
-March 1978

By the time Beverly and I left Orange County California it was about 10:00pm. After driving around for about 45 minutes we reached Los Angeles. From here I decided that in order to head back to Milwaukee, Wisconsin, we had to take the northern route. For me this was not an unusual route to take because I have made this drive many times in the past when I was younger. I had not driven this route when it was cold though.

This was the first time Beverly truly had ever been out of California. I think that this is why she was so excited about the trip. The funny thing is Beverly acted as if she knew where she was going. Little did I know that Beverly had a lot of issues and problems, which I was soon to find out about.

As we continued to drive we hit Utah. We had been up all night since I was doing all of the driving I started to get very tired and cranky. I could not understand where Beverly was getting all of her energy because she talked all night without stopping. In fact, all of the talking was driving me crazy so I wanted to pull over and get some rest.

When we finally did pull over Beverly asked someone for directions for Zion Park. Even after we received these directions we drove for hours and still got lost. Finally we finally did find Zion Park. When we did, it was early in the morning and the sun was starting to come out.

As we watched the sun rise we noticed that we were not alone anymore. We saw a crowd of people around us. After checking out the surroundings further, we realized that the people around us were actually Indians that lived in the area. They were praying and enjoying the sun rise.

Once the sun was completely out we decided to get back to our trip.

Again we drove for hours and got lost. About early evening we finally hit the main highway again. We gassed up the car, picked up some food, and continued to drive all night again.

Around 11:30pm we made it through a rough ice storm and to Vail, Colorado. When we reached Vail we decided to catch a meal and rest for a bit. We stayed in Vail for a couple of hours before hitting the road again. Once rested, we started back on the highway eighty the road to Milwaukee, Wisconsin again. We drove until about 8:00am until we stopped again. This time when we stopped we pulled to the side of the road.

By this time the weather was starting to warm up. We both were so exhausted so we decided to lie on top of the car. As the day grew longer the weather got warmer. We both received about 6 hours of rest before it started to get very cold again. As we woke up from the coldness we got back into the car and headed out of Colorado. Once outside of Colorado we passed some hitchhikers. Beverly wanted me to pick them up but I felt deeply against it. We did pick them up anyway and kept on driving.

Shortly after being with our new passengers we started to get high on marijuana. Beverly shared her medications for a few joints. Boy did I ever get wasted. I remained this way for quite a while. Then the unexpected happened. The right front axle of our car completely broke in half while we were driving. When this happened I just about freaked out. I also became very paranoid but I think that this was mainly from being so wasted.

We were all very lucky to barely make it off of the main freeway. I got out of the car, grabbed my clothes with my backpack and decided to start hitching on my own without Beverly. When I made this decision I actually started to feel better. By this time Beverly dropped her clothes and caught up with me. Now we both had to hitchhike to complete our trip.

We must have walked for about 30 minutes before we received a ride. By this time we were already in Illinois and more than two thirds of the way to our destination. All I knew is that I couldn't wait until we were finally able to completely stop and get some real food and rest again.

The ride that we received was from some truck drivers. They picked us up because Beverly was with me. They also wanted her and I knew it but because of the situation I could not do much about it. This is why I chose to just keep my mouth shut and go along for the ride.

The truck drivers fed us, got us high, and put us up in a room for about 3 days. During this time I almost had a job driving a truck with them but the opportunity did not pan out. In fact, the situation ended up getting pretty bad so one of the truck drivers suggested that we leave. That is when we started hitching again.

This time as we hitched it took us hours to get a ride. By evening it was very cold and the wind was blowing right through us. The worst wind that we experienced was in Chicago, Illinois while walking on a bridge. Finally we received a ride that took us all of the way to Milwaukee, Wisconsin.

Once in Milwaukee, I called my brother Tom. I told him what I was doing and because Beverly was with me, he decided to help us out for a couple of days. I took him up on his offer. (The thing is I also felt that I was opposing on him and his family). Eventually he set us up in a one-room apartment above a bar with a weeks' rent already paid.

While living above the bar, Beverly started to have seizures. I didn't know about these because she had never shared that she had a medical problem. When I first saw them I freaked out. I didn't know what to do so this is when I called 911.

Later I found out Beverly was an Epileptic and had stopped taking her medication while we were making our trip. Now I had another responsibility. This was to make sure Beverly took her medications. In the process I also had to learn how to care for Beverly when she had her seizures.

We had only lived in this new place above the bar for about a week when one of my uncles dropped in for a drink. When he saw me I said hi to him and we talked for a bit about old times. He then realized that I was broke and paid our rent for another week.

Shortly after we started to live in this new place Beverly continued to have frequent episodes of seizures. As I already mentioned at first I freaked out but then my confidence came back and we managed.

I was exhausted from our trip and I did not want to take the responsibility for caring for Beverly so I checked myself into a psyche hospital for a 72 hour hold. Beverly figured out how to visit me and did so. I wanted Beverly to also seek help but this did not happen. At this point I was messed up but I never felt that I was bad enough to stay for a long period of time so after the 72 hours I went back home.

After being in Milwaukee for about a couple of weeks I was able to start driving a taxicab again. This time when I did I started to make enough for both of us to live. I even took Beverly with me a few times so she could get a feel for the city and how to get around in the area we lived in.

This job lasted only lasted only a couple of months. I stopped driving because I was very close to loosing my drivers' license. When this happened I hooked up with the welfare system again and started in a rehab program. While looking for work, I was receiving money. The amount was not very much but for now that was okay. I stayed on the welfare program for a few more months.

We lived above the bar for a total of 4 months. While living there I had one of my friends over one night. He was one of the employee's I helped train when I managed at the Malings shoe store.

During the visit I found out that he was gay and he invited us out one evening. While he was visiting he witnessed Beverly having multiple seizures. When he saw these he realized that I had my hands full. A couple weeks later we did go out to a gay bar and had a very good time.

During those 4 months were able to save some money. Beverly was able to get her SSI restarted so we bought a car and moved into a 1-bedroom apartment. We were even able to furnish the apartment with new furniture.

Just before moving in though I had to go to court. The reason is because my divorce was going to finally be finalized. I was glad about this and felt that it was about time.

While at court Bambi was there. She was with her attorney talking about me and putting me down. She didn't realize I was there because she only remembered me as a guy with a military haircut. Having Beverly there for support on my part confused her.

Shortly after court Bambi asked us for a ride. Of course we gave it to her because we were going to see our daughter Tammy Lynn.

I did feel uncomfortable about the visit. I remember that Tammy Lynn did too because I had someone new with me and she had not seen me for a long time. Beverly did break the ice and the visit ended up going well. We even had another visit shortly after this one.

Our new neighbors were very friendly and helpful. When I was at work one of the boys stayed and played cards with Beverly. It was the summer so this young man watching out for Beverly worked out very well.

Those summer days in Milwaukee sure were hot. I remember having a major water fight in our kitchen. We completely flooded the floor and it took forever to clean the mess up. Getting soaked sure was fun though.

After living at our new place for about a month Beverly finally contacted her parents. This time her dad was more receptive to her. Apparently Beverly had asked her dad for some money without asking me first. I really didn't care because she was at least talking to her parents again.

Living with Beverly was hell because she would always strike out at me prior to having one of her seizures. To me this was too much so I was actually glad to be away from her at work.

Beverly had a lot of problems. She married very young and was in the drug scene at an early age and for quite a while. This is when she hung with the Timothy O'Leary group when they were in Laguna Hills, California. Her first husband would physically abuse her and almost killed her by banging her head into a concrete wall many times.

Until that time Beverly would keep everything hidden from her dad for fear that her dad would physically kill this husband. When she left that marriage she became a prostitute, an alcoholic, and drug abuser. She would pull tricks to support her own habits and to live. This is when she started to have seizures.

During that time she decided to keep everything suppressed inside. By doing so she found various personalities within herself. For many years these personalities controlled her life.

If you remember I met Beverly in California. At that time I did not know that she had a bunch of personalities and baggage. All I knew is that she was different and that she liked me.

I worked with Beverly 1-to-1 and found out that she had about at least 10 personalities. These were all based on a lifestyle that she wanted to forget and the drug scene she had lived in a good part of her adult life. This is why we would have a lot of our arguments and physical fights.

We would spend hours each day trying to piece her life history together. Doing so seemed like it took forever and those fights did not make it any easier. Beverly created multiple personalities to deal with new situations and environments. Eventually these personalities completely took over her life and she forgot who she really was. The whole process of piecing this entire story together took about 8-months of one-to-one communication and a lot of violence.

Once I had the story, I shared what he knew with Beverly. When it looked like Beverly discovered and accepted what happened she started to become one single person again. The sad part is as improvement happened with Beverly, the violence did not stop because she was very stubborn. The improvements started to appear only after I found personalities within my self that could match hers. Eventually after a lot of time Beverly dropped her personalities and accepted who she was and what she had been through.

By the end of July and the beginning of August I landed a job as a security guard. I worked the night shift as a security guard at a foundry in Cudahay, Wisconsin. The position lasted until about December. This is when I decided I had enough again and I wanted to head back to California.

Due to me being upset at the time about the job, I had Beverly intervene. She ended up cursing out my bosses prior to us leaving Wisconsin. Shortly after she did this we packed up our car, grabbed our saved money, and started to head back to California.

On the Road to California again
December 1978

We started out in our Pontiac Catalina early in the afternoon. This time we decided to try to drove straight through. Our only stops were for gasoline, food, and use of the restroom. Beverly was not as talkative during the drive this time, so it seemed like we reached Colorado in no time.

By the time we reached Colorado the car a 1988 Catalina, started to run rough and made a lot of noise. I knew that it would not make to California so I decided to sell it.

Beverly wanted to hitchhike again because she had fun doing so the last time that we did. I did not want to hitchhike. I just wanted to make it back to California as soon as possible and in one piece.

I already was exhausted with dealing with and being responsible for Beverly all of these months. I also still had my own issues to deal with. Due to my taking this responsibility I buried these problems. Once we sold the car I figured that we would have just enough to complete our trip and have some meals.

We used some of our money to take a Greyhound bus and the rest for meals. Our trip to Santa Ana, California took us about 2 ½ days but it seemed like it took longer. We arrived in Santa Ana, California at about 9:30pm.

As soon as we got off of the bus and gathered our belongings, Beverly tried to call her parents. She was unable to reach them.

Since we still had some money left we climbed into a taxicab and went over to her parent's home. Once we arrived at her parent's home we were immediately accepted. In fact, all of us stayed up until wee hours in the morning.

Beverly and I shared as much as we could remember about our trip and stay in Milwaukee, Wisconsin. We also had a good home cooked meal. By the time we were ready for bed, I was thanked for taking care of Beverly and bringing her back home.

Living in California Again!

As I said above we arrived into California on an early evening in December. After getting to Beverly's' family's home only 30 minutes we talked, ate, and went to bed in the wee hours of the morning. Even then I was too keyed up to sleep, so Beverly and I sat up and talked for a couple more hours.

We were lucky enough to sleep in the next day. No matter what time I went to sleep the night before, I still was up by about 10:00am. Beverly and her mom ended up sleeping in all of the way until the early afternoon.

This was great because it gave Beverly's dad and I an opportunity to get to know each other better. It also gave me the chance to learn more about Beverly, mainly before I met her about 10 months prior.

Through our conversation I realized that the information that Beverly and I put together was pretty accurate. By this time Beverly and her mom finally woke up.

All of us had a wonderful afternoon and evening together. It was good food, good conversation, and just good company. We also sat down and played some cards.

Late in the evening Beverly's parents talked about going on a trip for a couple of weeks toward the end of the year. This is when they asked us to watch their home while they were away. Of course we agreed to do so without any hesitation.

The next week went by very quickly. When Jack and Eunice left for their vacation, we were left at home to watch the place.

I could not stand just staying at home, so I went out job hunting. Finally I did find a job with Alltel Telephone Products Incorporated. I was going to work on the assembly line. When I didn't work on the line

I would be helping out pulling out stock for the line. I was to start this new position after January 1, 1979.

The couple of weeks that Jack and Eunice took for vacation went by very quickly. When they arrived back home they were surprised to see that I had already found a job. Jack was so pleased that he helped us find a car so I could get to work without any problems. We also talked about the direction that we thought that the job market would be going here in California. Both of us came to the decision that working with computers was the direction to go and the way of the future.

Once this was decided, I went to Santa Ana College to sign up for a Electronic Technology Program. Since I was a veteran I also signed up for a tuition assistance program, which meant we would have extra income each month I stayed enrolled three-fourths time or 9 units a semester.

By the time February 1979 came around, I was already in school and we had moved out of Beverly's parent's home into a 1-bedroom apartment. I worked for Alltel a telecommunications company for a couple of months and then landed a better position with Computer Automation.

Being with this new company allowed me to learn about building computers which coincided with the courses I had already been taking. I started out on the assembly line and moved to the hot solder flow machine operator position. I actually learned this position within a month and got pretty good at it.

The work was tedious and when things were slow I was responsible for cleaning this machine and preparing it for the next day. To me the work was boring and not what I wanted to do in the future. I wanted to be a computer technician or even an engineer.

While I was working Beverly would be at home. She would talk with our neighbors and at times would barrow money from them. Barrowing money from others is something that I really hated. This is why when I found out about the barrowing, we would end up getting into huge fights. Many times when I would come home and I did not know where to find her. We would have knockdown fights and we would end up hitting and hurting each other. These arguments would happen a lot and when Beverly did not get her way she would attempt to commit suicide by overdosing on her regularly ordered medication. When she did this it really bothered me and at times I had to leave just to settle down and pull myself together.

One day when I was at work working with solder machine, things were not going very well for me. I kept burning the bottoms of the circuit boards. My mind was not on my work because of everything that had been happening in the past and at home. All of this just kept building up on me and I kept everything to myself. I ended up having a true nervous breakdown and had to have an ambulance take me from work to the hospital. While at the hospital I was seen by the Psychiatric Emergency Team (PET). They admitted me immediately to the Benjamin Rush Center, which was part of St. Joseph's Hospital in Orange, California.

At first I was placed on a 72-hour hold for observation. This ended up becoming longer because I had a problem with adjusting to the environment around me. I would cry about almost any little thing.

My treatment consisted of medication, various group therapies and assertive training, a bunch of tests including biofeedback. Most of my days were full with all of these. Finally after being in the hospital about 3 weeks, I was released on a pass. The idea was to see if I could return to society and possibly back to work.

I was not as ready as I thought I should be because when I went to where I was staying prior to being in the hospital. I broke down into tears again and an ambulance had to bring me back to the hospital. Eventually I was released from the hospital after being there for over 6-8 weeks.

During my hospital stay I was tried on at least 4 different types of antidepressant medications. Most of these medications caused me to have some type of reaction. Finally I was started on Senaquan and I was also informed that in order to completely stabilize I would have to do follow-up care as an outpatient for at least one year. One thing I did find out about myself while I was in the hospital was that I was truly a bisexual. My bisexualism was defined by the role I was living at the time (or so I thought). I also discovered that I could even be a transsexual that would possibly be transitioning within the next 15 years. Of course this last one I was not sure about because I was in denial about who I was in the first place. I did follow-up with outside therapy as recommended and I returned back to work shortly after. This time I actually did work in the assembly area.

I lived by myself for the first couple of weeks after the hospitalization.

This was very hard for me to do because I still was not 100% emotionally stable yet. In fact, during this time period I had considered starting my sexual transitioning from male-to-female. I even started to do so by wearing some woman's clothing beneath my male clothing and in public on my days off.

About a month after returning back to work Beverly ended up back in my life. A couple of weeks to a month later we ended up marrying. We lived in a small one-room apartment in one of the poorest parts of town. Again Beverly stayed at home while I worked. She got to know all of our neighbors again. She also saved the drawings I had done when I was in the hospital. We ended up framing most of them and hanging the in our small place.

Married Again! Marriage (Strike 2)
1979

The day we got married we both were very nervous. I was so bad that I had to get high just to make this happen for me. Beverly did the same. The wedding was successful and we both enjoyed that day.

The first few months of marriage were pretty calm. Beverly and I did get along even in the tiny single bachelor type apartment that we lived in. I continued to work for Computer Automation through January 1980.

While doing so we were able to save up our money again and moved into a nice 1-bedroom apartment in Tustin, California. This is when we started to have our knock down and drag down fights again. It got so bad that Beverly's dad threatened to hurt me if I continued to lay a hand on his daughter.

During this time Beverly continued to try to hurt herself by overdosing on her pills, cutting herself, or trying to hang herself. She even was treated several times in the hospital for some of these attempts.

She would continue to have her epileptic seizures more frequently because she would forget to take her medications so I ended up monitoring her medications again as I did in Wisconsin. This bothered me a lot, because I still was not all that stable. I was still seeing a psychiatrist at least once a week and on medication.

Besides having our own problems to deal with we tried to help out others we remember from living in the streets. Of course how could we help others when we were barely caring for ourselves?

By the end summer 1980 I moved from Computer Automation to Silicon Systems. I started here as a microchip tester. I started to like this job, but I knew that this was only a stepping-stone to the type of position I really wanted to do. That was the position of computer technician. This is why I continued on with my classes at Santa Ana College.

While I was in school taking classes I was too busy to deal with my own feelings and problems. I was very stressed out about everything that had been happening in my life. I did find time to cross-dress though. For me this was a type of stress relief that I would resort back to when things got very tough in my life. Of course most of this cross-dressing would always be hidden or when no one was home. I also kept these episodes mostly to myself and refused to discuss them or would deny I had this problem when caught dressed.

When all of this was going on Beverly started to get closer to her sister again. In fact, all of us spent a lot of good times together partying. Shortly after this happened, I was able to piece more of Beverly's history together, which was scary, because I was not sure about what I was getting myself into. By late summer of 1980 we moved from our 1-bedroom apartment to a house located also in Tustin.

Near the end of 1981 Beverly had been in the hospital several times for trying to commit suicide. She also had her oldest son move in with us, which was a real disaster. I finally had become stabilized with my medications and dealing somewhat with my own feelings. I still was not brave enough to let Beverly know what was truly going on with my cross-dressing and me.

When she was in the hospital in December, I found out that my middle brother was killed while he was stationed in Holland serving with the United States Army. Shortly after hearing this I was very upset and shocked. I knew that I had to plan an emergency trip to Florida, and have Beverly accompany me since we were married and because I could not trust her when she was completely alone.

I think that the part that upset me the most about the trip was that he was going to be buried on my birthday December 18th. I continued to coordinate everything to get Beverly out of the hospital and made arrangements for our trip. We arrived in Orlando, Florida on the 16th of December.

Shortly after arriving we dropped off our baggage at my parent's home. Then all of us headed out to eat before viewing my younger brother's remains. My folks treated us to a smorgasbord type meal first.

By about 7:00pm we headed for the funeral parlor storing my brother's remains. When looking at him his face looked battered as if he had his nose broken. This was very obvious to all of us. He also looked like he had other injuries, many of which were covered up by the United States Army.

After viewing his remains we headed home. My brothers were in tears. They could not believe this had happened. They also started drinking beer and were feeling sorry for themselves.

I personally was very withdrawn into my own protective shell. I think I did this because I still had a lot on my plate and I was still on edge. I also had my own problems with cross-dressing and being bisexual that my family never knew about. I was not going to let them know all of this right now since we just lost a family member. There was even the problem dealing with Beverly. This is why I resorted to practicing my Kung Fu moves and why I worked on my carta's or Kung Fu practice moves.

On my birthday December 18, 1981 we buried my brother. During the ceremony my dad, mom, and others in our family were in tears. I personally did not because my relationship with my brother Mark was pressured and distant. I think mainly so because he would always ask for my advise and ask me a lot of questions. Later I found out that my dad responded the way he did because Mark was the middle son and he was the middle son in his family.

The army paid for Mark's funeral with casket and everything but they still hid information from my family. He also received a 21-gun salute. If he had committed suicide as someone told our family, this whole thing would have been paid out of our pocket. They also would not have paid out on his life insurance. Beverly and I stayed with my folks through Christmas.

The rest of our visit went well and we did have a good time. Tammy Lynn (my daughter) stayed mostly to herself during the whole visit. Beverly was able to interact with her, but she refused to interact with me. I believe that the reason is because she already was very angry with me for what I had done with her when she was younger.

My mom had me sign paperwork to place Tammy on welfare. I didn't know why, because they had offered to care for her in the first place. Later I found out that this was their intension all along. I especially found this out when I had to start paying child support back to the state of Florida and then regular child support.

Beverly and I made it back to California without any problems. When we got back we found out that her oldest son had broken one of the main windows in the house we were renting. He apparently has a party there when we were gone without our permission. Once I found this out I had enough and kicked him out shortly thereafter.

At the end of the summer of 1983 I finally left Silicon Systems Incorporated. This was after working as a computer technician for about 3-4 months. I found that I was not catching on as well as I thought I was even after I had completed my associate's degree that spring.

I went from this position to Ford Aerospace as a tester. The bad thing about this job is that a security clearance was needed and I wasn't sure if I had a record. This new position only lasted about a month and I was laid off. I think I was really fired because again I was not catching on with the electronics portion of the position.

A Career Change, Becoming a Nurse

After being laid off I decided to fall back on my military background. I enrolled in a review course with a Licensed Vocational Nurse (LVN) Program. The program lasted 3 months. Once completing this part of the program I received my Certified Nurses Aide (CNA) Credential and started to work as a CNA for an agency. I did so until I was able to find a position with an acute hospital setting. Finding the position happened by January of 1984. Until that point I continued to work as an agency CNA and would ride my Honda Hawk Hondamatic motorcycle to my jobs that were usually near Tustin and Irvine, California.

In January 1984 I started working as a CNA on an orthopedic floor during the night shift at Fountain Valley Regional Medical Center. I was the only CNA caring for about 45 patients on this unit. I learned the routine quickly and the Registered Nurses (RN) helped me as much as possible. I absorbed what they taught me like a sponge.

While working in this position I was awaiting to take the LVN boards. By April 1984 I did take those LVN boards and passed. I finally became a LVN. The RN's I worked with threw me a party shortly after this happened.

When I tried to work with Fountain Valley Regional Medical Center as a LVN, they did not want to work with me. They wanted me to continue to work as a CNA and not get the experience I needed as a LVN. I felt that this was not fair so I moved on without having a new position to fall back on.

I did find a position at Western Medical Center Bartlett located in Orange California. Now I could get the experience I need as a nurse.

During orientation I proved I could handle the acute floor position. I was able absorb what I was taught in the couple of weeks of classroom and on hands training.

I also showed that I could manage the toughest patients with minimal problems. I was then moved to the night shift as a charge nurse on one of the toughest units in the facility. I continued to learn from my peers and had a very good report with my immediate supervisor. She continued to teach me new procedures and eventually I was on my own.

During this time I continued to have many problems with Beverly. We would still fight a lot. I knew that our relationship would soon end. I also knew that it would only be a matter of time.

This is when I started to wear earrings in both ears and female clothing under my uniforms. No one suspected what I was doing because I still was able to carry myself as a male nurse and in a professional manner when I was working.

The CNA's I worked with began to hate me. The reason is because I would require them to do more than 2-3 rounds per night. I also would require them to do extras that they should really have been doing on their own in the first place. This is why I was lucky to have the support of my immediate supervisor. They eventually did do the work that I asked them to do under duress.

Instead of dealing with my feelings I concentrated on the work I was doing. I also went back to my old crutch of drinking alcohol on my days off. I even would go back to my cross-dressing (still mostly hidden of course) more often. There were times I worked overtime after having a few beers, which I should not have done.

I would carry myself as if I was always angry when I worked. Part of this was because I did not have a release for my feelings other than my cross-dressing. My supervisor was a partial release but during this time in my life I only shared bits and pieces. I never truly shared everything about what was happening in my life.

By late 1985 a RN by the name of Susan was hired on the 3-11 shift. She was to be the new Charge Nurse on the Sub-acute unit (the unit I worked during the night shift). I met her as I was coming on to my 11-7 shift.

When I met her we hit it off. I think that the main reason is because we were close to being the same age. She must have realized that I was lonely and needed someone to talk too.

Susan was a new RN at the time, and she was very knowledgeable. After giving me a report when she completed her shift, she would stay over to talk with me even though she was married with three children. She would also do another shift to help us out because we had times when we were very short of nurses. This is when we realized that we were very competitive as nurses. We saw this many times and I tried to learn from her while competing against her.

Around this time I had just about had it with being with Beverly. I know part of the reason is because Beverly had improved dramatically by starting to work as a manager at a photo shop. We had moved from a house back into an apartment. I became jealous of her much of the time so that I decided to try to work part time for her.

At first I tried working as a telemarketer and found that I was not good on the telephone. I then decided to help out delivering the pictures and as a collector. I would do so on my 400cc Honda Hawk Hondamatic motorcycle.

I got pretty good at these deliveries. I think that this happened because I was able to make the deliveries fairly quickly. I also drove this motorcycle too fast. Finally the fast driving caught up with me. I had an accident when I was driving 94 MPH and tried to slow down to quickly. When I hit the ground I wiped out the faring and signal lights of the motorcycle. If I had not been wearing a vinyl/leather jacket and a helmet I would have torn up my upper body and hit my head. After the accident I decided that delivering pictures was not for me.

By the early part of 1986 Susan and I started to get a lot closer and see each other. We would sneak off after work and started to kiss and pet. When it was slow we would even try to kiss and talk while we were at work. Eventually we would end up having sexual intercourse.

I knew when this happened that for me my life with Beverly was about to completely end. The final clincher was when Beverly went to a party without inviting me. She never did come home that evening so I went out looking for and never did find her. I later found out that Beverly was back on cocaine again and that she had an affair of her own. When I found this out I decided that I was going to leave her forever. The reason is because when we first got married I informed her that if you go back to drugs that we would be through. My jealousy also got the best of me and in this case it was justified. I was true to my word.

The day I decided to leave I didn't completely think everything through. I had Susan help me gather my things. I ended up only taking my clothes and left everything else behind.

Since I didn't have a place to stay yet she offered to have me stay in her home until I got settled. Of course I took her up on her offer and stayed on the couch in the family room of their house.

Susan had to have outpatient surgery shortly after I moved in. The same day of the surgery Susan and I had intercourse. We then sat and talked about potential plans of moving in together. Our decision was to have me find a place first, prove that I could live on my own, and she would join me soon after. I ended up staying in this home until the next payday, which was only in a couple of weeks. Of course Susan and I spent as much time as possible together.

I remember that I installed a used radio in one of her cars before I moved out. The project took me about 4 hours because it had been such a long time since I had worked with my electronics. The radio also didn't quite fit so I had to modify the dash to make it fit. When I was done everything worked very well and Susan was very pleased with the job I did. Eventually I moved into a bachelor apartment close to Susan's home.

While on my own I considered possibly transitioning so a lot of cross-dressing took place more frequently when I was home alone. Of course Susan did not know any of this because I never shared it with her. I just kept everything to myself as I had done in the past. Doing so was hard to do but since I had been hiding this so long it didn't seen to bad.

Shortly after moving into my new place I left Western Medical Center Bartlett and started working at Western Neuro Center. Susan would come by after she got done working at Western Medical Center Bartlett at times. We would continue to have sex when she did. Eventually Susan did move in with me.

For the first couple of months Susan had to pay child support. The reason is because she left the marriage. Finally near her 4th month living with me she was able to stop paying the support. It was summer by this time and we were able to see her 3 children more. This was hard on me because we had 5 of us living in a very small apartment and I became clusterphobic.

The summer went by quickly. When her children started back to school I also decided to start taking my perquisites for the RN program. Susan offered to help me by proof reading my assignments.

I remember when I started the RN program that I had a very hard time with my spelling and grammar. This is why I had Susan proof read everything I wrote. Sometimes she had to read what I wrote at least 5-10 times and I ended up rewriting many of these papers . There were times that I had to rewrite my papers at least 10 times too. When this happened it seemed like it took forever just to get just one assignment done.

By October of 1986 Susan's divorce was finalized. That same day that she received her finalized divorce papers we went to the courthouse and obtained a marriage license. Shortly after we did this we got married.

Marriage #3
1986.

At the time that we got married I really wasn't ready. I say this because of the previous violent marriage that I just got out of. Susan also was very bossy which threw me off. I did not expect this at all. I did go along with it though mainly because she had been helping me with my RN classes and I did care for her a lot. For me the honeymoon of being married was over.

By November we were looking into buying a home. All that we could qualify for was a 3-bedroom condominium. We figured that I could use my GI Bill for financing. The whole process took us about a month. By this time I had finished my prerequisites and by spring 1987 I started in the accelerated LVN-to-RN program with Golden West College.

During the first term I had a problem with maintaining my grades and working full time. I think part of the problem was related to the stress of a ready-made family and because I still was taking prerequisite classes.

I did make it through until the last 2 weeks of the program before I had to stop and retake the course. The soonest I could start again was in the fall. In order to be ready for the fall term I would have to take a couple of courses during the summer. These courses will help me understand the areas I had my weaknesses in when I was in the program the previous semester.

I also visited with Beverly's parents Jack and Eunice. They informed me that Beverly had succeeded at committing suicide. She overdosed on Inderal pills and alcohol. The final autopsy showed that Beverly aspirated causing aspiration pneumonia secondary to her overdose. We came to the conclusion that when Beverly drank the alcohol after she took the pills that she might have had an epileptic seizure. Beverly was 38 years old when this happened. She also had been giving things away and was saying good-bye to everybody prior to her demise.

Two of Susan's children moved in with us. Their names were Daniel and Shannon. Little did I know that having 2 children in the house would cause chaos. These 2 children were always arguing and there were many times when Susan fed into their arguments and she would yell back. This did not help my concentration and added to the stress I was already experiencing from my courses. Off course I started to cross-dress again which added to my stress.

The fall term came quickly. This time I was bettered prepared. I saw this when I was able to maintain A and B grades in my classes. I completed the first semester of the program with very minimal problems.

During this first semester we studied about various psychological problems. Besides receiving the theory we were able experience what we were taught in the clinical setting. I found through this experience that I did pretty well. I think the reason is because I had actually been a patient and on medication in the past.

My daughter Tammy Lynn made a surprise visit by driving out for a visit. She drove from Florida straight through within 24 hours. Having her visit was great. I remember spoiling her by buying her some new clothes and one of our local malls. I even tried to have a talk with her but that failed. Susan, her children and I even took a picture with her during this visit.

The spring semester went by quickly. A lot of what we were taught was a review on what I learned in the training to be a LVN. The same was true with the clinical aspect of the course. In fact, I was able to show my background and experience by excelling ahead of some of my peers.

During the last 1½ months of the course I ended up getting tired. The reason is because there were quite a few days that I only was able to get very little sleep. My motivation for hanging in was that I knew that the situation was only a temporary one and that I would have completed the course.

By April 1988 I graduated and I was glad because I was tired of training new graduates and not getting paid for it. Shortly after I graduated I applied for my Interim RN permit and received it. Once I received this I quit Western Neuro and started working at Saint Joseph's hospital located on Orange, California. This was the same hospital that Susan had moved to when she left Western Medical Center Bartlett.

The unit I worked was the telemetry or CORE unit. I would also float to the surgical and medical units as a RN. I took the RN boards in November 1988. When I took the RN boards the first time I did not pass. This meant that I lost my Interim permit and had to resume the duties a LVN. For me this did not work out because I kept being floated.

For a while I was even in the Emergency room working. They decided to terminate me because I was not quick enough. With these two things happening so close together I was devastated. The main reason is because I wanted to do my share with raising our family. Everything did work out because I was able to land a position with Cost Care Healthcare Services on the day shift. This was a day shift position.

The first month at this position my hours were from 8:00am until 5:00pm. The reason for this was because the training was on various screens related to assessments and telephone intakes. I was lucky again because I had my computer background, but with this type of position it was not the same. By the end of the first month I finally did catch on and I was assigned to an intake group that started by 6:00am.

Getting up by about 5am was initially hard for me. It took me at least 2 months to adjust to this early schedule. When I did adjust I found that I was already having problems with being too hard on the nurses giving me information for authorization of their patient's hospital stay.

Around this same time I also started to get more involved with Calvary Chapel Costa Mesa Church. I became reborn and was baptized by submersion in the Pacific Ocean by Pastor Chuck Smith.

As I studied the bible I really absorbed what I read. I had a problem with memorizing scripture, but I was able to find where various scriptures were. I was also capable of making my own interpretation on what I read.

By 1989 I was able to quit smoking as a New Years resolution. I knew that in April I would be repeating the RN boards. This is when I contacted Dr. Vernon Farley the Dean of the nursing program at Golden West College in Huntington Beach, California. She offered me a complete set of study tapes that would be helpful for these RN boards. This time I also took a review course a few days before taking these boards. I even took thousands of nursing test questions, which gave me a better chance of passing and used the review tapes at least 10 times.

When I did take the RN boards this time I was more prepared. I even kept up with all of the areas I was being tested on. At times I completed different sections of ahead of my peers. This surprised me and due to these results I felt that I either passed at a high level, or failed drastically. The outcome was that I passed with a very high score.

About a month after I took these RN boards Susan had our son. She was upset at me because initially I had asked her to abort this child early in her pregnancy. When he was born all of these thoughts changed and I tried to be more supportive with Susan. The thing is she chose to concentrate on raising Joshua Michael Joseph Powalisz mostly by herself. Our relationship started to pull apart shortly after this happened.

About a month or two after Josh was born I decided to check into getting myself fixed. I planned for a vasectomy. Having this procedure upset Susan even more because she wanted to have more children. I felt that the world was too cruel and corrupt to bring another child into this world.

Once I passed the RN boards I went back to Fountain Valley Regional Medical Center. While there I started working the 11-7 shift again on a Step-down unit. Because I was considered a new RN, I also ended up floating to the medical floor, which was the old orthopedic floor I had worked at when I was a CNA. I worked at this hospital for about a year and then found a better position at Western Medical Center Santa Ana. I wanted to specialize in the ICU so I signed up for a 3-month program.

The Critical Care course was tough. This was because of the way that the material was taught and the expectations. At first I was not catching on but toward the end of the program I was able to complete the program. After completing the program I transferred to Western Medical Center Anaheim.

During the first few months in this facility I worked as a charge nurse on the medical-surgical-telemetry floor. I even floated to the ICU. When I did float I found out that they were short on nurses so I ended up floating a lot. I also applied for the open position and got it.

It took me about 3 months to learn the unit. Once I did I had occasions when I was placed in charge. I even became proficient at the position because Pilipino nurses taught me. They showed me all of the tricks and of course I absorbed everything like a sponge again.

In 1991 I was asked to give my daughter Tammy Lynn away at her first wedding. My dad was also asked to do so because he had helped to raise her. Susan, Daniel, Shannon, Joshua, and I made the trip to Orlando, Florida for this occasion.

On the night before the wedding I could not sleep. I ended up staying up all night reading the book Psalms. Tammy's best friend sat up with me and we discussed the bible all night.

By the time of the wedding and the reception I was completely exhausted. I even saw that I was very stiff. This I saw when I danced with Tammy. The wedding was another enjoyable time for all of us.

Once we returned back to California for me things were not the same. When Susan was not at home I went back to my cross-dressing again. There were even times when I almost go caught.

When Susan found my stash of hidden woman's clothing and asked me about them I denied that they were mine. I blamed them on her son Daniel saying that he was experimenting. Initially she accepted this answer, but I knew that eventually she didn't believe me.

Susan and I kept going into debt. This is when I decided to get a second job. Working 2 jobs was my way of escaping from the family. Now I was never at home to help raise my little boy. I also went back into the military as a nurse with the reserves. I believe that this even upset Susan even more.

By 1994 I decided to pursue my Bachelor's Degree in nursing. We invested in a home computer and a laptop to help me get through my courses. This time I did not ask Susan for her assistance. These investments were made because I did not want to go through the typing and retyping I went through when I obtained my Associates Degree in 1988.

I spent many hours working on my assignments. Besides working on these assignments I also would stay on the computer for hours at a time. This really upset Susan because we no longer had meaningful conversations.

When we visited her family she would become more critical of me. Even after the visits we would argue more. Of course I hated to argue so

I just avoided and ignored some of these arguments which made Susan even more upset.

To me this was being hypicritical. I could not see faking it as if everything was okay when it really wasn't. Susan never saw this. She tried to warn me that eventually she would not be with me. She even said to me that we would not be growing old together. "You are going to be alone and angry."

During this time my cross-dressing increased even more. Susan would find my clothes more often and of course I would lie to her as I did in the past. It is as if I wanted to be caught. When it got close for me it was a rush.

I did finally finish my degree by April of 1997. Shortly after this Susan decided to have some facial surgery done. I was there for her during the surgery and she appreciated it (so I thought). She paid for the surgery by hiding money from me. Of course I never knew how much because she was the one who managed our finances.

During the time that I was getting my BSN degree I was in in the U. S. Army Reserves. I worked in the reserves once a month while holding down 2 jobs. I started at the rank of second lieutenant. Because I remained very dedicated, I made it all of the way to the rank of captain.

While in the reserves I served in Panama and in northern California during annual training. As I was at training Susan was already cheating on me. In fact, one time I made a surprise visit home and she was not there. When this happened I started to no longer trust her.

By the time summer came around I knew in my heart that Susan and I would soon get a divorce. I thought by changing my job and making more time for the family that everything would get better. Little did I realize that it was too late. I should have been there long before. Then the inevitable happened.

Divorce Again! Trauma/Strike #3

In November 1997 I found out from a neighbor that Susan had been having an affair. The whole thing had been going on with someone I had fired when I worked in Home Health. The sad thing is that it also had been going on for quite some time.

When this happened I freaked out. I didn't want to believe what I heard. That is why I had decided to confront Susan. By this time she had already stopped talking to me. When I did confront her she admitted to it but denied any sexual contact. Knowing our past history I knew that she was lying to me.

As soon as I heard my answer I was very devastated. I cracked. What bothered me the most is Susan was very cold to me and showed no emotions. I started to become angry with her to the point that I started to strike out at her. This reaction at the time was very unusual for me. I say this because no matter how much we argued in the past Susan and I had never laid a hand on each other.

The whole incident made Susan afraid of me. So much so that she gathered up Joshua and decided to go to her moms home. I even tried to convince Josh at the time that all that happened between Susan and I was not his fault. Susan and Josh did leave. When this happened of course I was all alone.

Being alone lately has been hard for me even though I have been alone anyway these past years subconsciously. Now everything has surfaced and I had to face it and myself first hand. Under the present circumstances all of this made me uncomfortable. It also made me severely depressed. This is when I started to do a lot of soul searching.

To date I had thought that everything was going better in my life. I cut back my hours at work. I was going to be home more often so that I could be with the family more. And I finally was going to make enough money to support my family. The problem is all of this was too late. I say this because I was loosing everything when I lost my family.

Yes, I placed the guilt and burden of all of this on my own shoulders. I psychologically started to beat myself up. Due to the circumstances and situation I had another nervous breakdown. I was more depressed than I had ever been in the past. Terrible thoughts were racing through my mind. Some of these thoughts were of even taking my own life again.

One evening when I was home alone I had planned to kill myself by using a butcher knife. I was going to cut my wrists and also stab myself in the chest right through my heart. I ended up praying all night and by early morning something stopped me. I decided to live my life now for me.

At first I thought that it was my self-preservation instinct. It could have been this, but today I believe that the reason I didn't succeed is because at this point and time I was not suppose to die. When I had these terrible feelings is when I started to pray to God. While I was praying I tried to bargain with Him. I denied that I had done anything wrong.

I was faced with the reality that for the longest time I had been a liar. I lied about so many things not only to Susan, but also to others in my life. The biggest lie I told is that I was completely straight; when in reality I was bisexual. I did lie to myself too.

This lie was that I had been dealing with my feelings honestly. The truth be told is that I for many years I would keep my true feelings inside. In a sense this is known as swallowing ones feelings, which is never healthy. I ended up staying up all of that night praying.

If I had stayed on the path I was going before I started my prayers, I would not be alive today. Through these prayers I realized that God is in control of everything. I had to put my faith back in Him. This is what I did; at least that is what I thought that I did at the time.

When all of this was going in my personal life I was in the middle of a job change. I was leaving American Home Health for more money. My new position was going to be as a Director with Staff Builders (Tender Loving Care) Home Health.

At first I felt that I was catching on to this new position. I received a cram course on doing Medicare/Medicaid admissions. I also made supervisory visits on cases that were already open. Some of these cases were very sick kids and poor families. The visits made an impact on me. So much so, that I became very sensitive and emotional.

When I came home from work one day I saw Susan in the kitchen. She was trying to replace the filter for the refrigerator but had no clue on how to do so. She was having a problem with it because she had bought the wrong filter. She also was not mechanically inclined so I went to the Home Depot and picked out the right filter.

When I got home I still was very emotional. I demonstrated to Susan how she made me feel by pulling out a butcher knife and pretending to stab myself in the heart. I then told her about what happened when I found out about her affair. She denied the sexual contact again but I still didn't believe her. I then broke down into tears right in front of her and again she was cold and showed no emotion. Shortly after I did this I left and talked with a fellow nurse I knew by the name of Carrie.

I had known Carrie for a while and remember doing some maintenance work for her. At one time she had worked for me when I was a Director with American Home Health and Hospice. In a sense I figured that she was a friend.

I told Carrie what I have just been through with Susan. She was great and tried to be supportive. She suggested that I go get some help because she saw that I was not handling everything very well and that I was having another nervous breakdown. Shortly after I talked with her I headed to Western Medical Center Anaheim where I had worked before. I was able to drive myself there.

Once at the hospital I completely broke into tears again. I could not regain my composure so a Psychiatric Evaluation Team (PET) member was called.

The evaluation showed that I was under stress and that I had a nervous breakdown. The nurse recommended that I get admitted for psychological treatment as an in-patient. I agreed to receive follow-up care as an outpatient.

The nurse and I talked with my immediate supervisor. A final decision was made for me to take off work for a day. I also had an appointment to meet with a psychiatrist the next day. Finally I was medicated with Ativan, which calmed me down enough to drive back home and get some sleep.

The next afternoon I did make my appointment and I was started on

Zoloft. The following day I went back to work. When I did this I closed as many credit cards and bank accounts as I could get completed by myself. Others weren't closed because they were joint accounts. I then tried to go out on a nursing supervisory visit. The visit was unsuccessful.

On my way coming home from this visit I was in tears again. This is when I met a paralegal John Tsamadas. I told him my story and what I had just been through.

John set me up with a new psychiatrist and an attorney. The next plan that John had was to get the paperwork put together for a divorce and new place for me to live. The cost of all of this was $10,000.00, which was to be paid up front.

We were able to get the money put together before the bank closed that Friday afternoon. At the time that all of this was going on I was so weak and unstable that I just made this transaction happen. I then went to my new place and got some sleep.

During the weekend when I met up with John we started working on the divorce paperwork. I actually did most of my own typing. John later brought in a friend of his to finish up. That night we did an all-nighter and by Sunday we had just about everything ready for court filing on Monday morning.

On November 13, 1998 I arrived at the residence where Susan was staying (my old town home) with a moving crew. The plan was to serve Susan her divorce papers and then remove what I wanted to keep from the home. Susan and I served each other divorce papers at the same time.

Immediately after this happened Susan tried to force her way past the moving truck and wrecked her van. I then called John and he told me to just move everything and that we would handle the service of the paper problem at another time.

Once she got by she headed to her mom's home. We then continue to load up the moving truck. Everything was moved out within about 4 hours. It took almost 5 more hours to move everything into the new place because my new place was upstairs. Shortly after all of this happened I headed off to bed.

Later during this same week I was laid off from my new nursing position. Now I had spent all of this money for this divorce and nothing really to show for these efforts. I also had totally demolished my only means of transportation, a red Nissan Sentra in an automobile accident.

Immediately after the accident I called John and he was able to get me into a 1995 T-bird by the end of that evening.

Through the rest of November and into December I started to help John out as a paralegal trainee. I also continued to see this new psychiatrist at least once a week. On December 24, 1998 while meeting with my psychiatrist, I ended up having another nervous breakdown. This time I ended up in a fetal position as I had in the 1970's.

I wanted to run away because everything I was going through right now was too tough for me to handle. When this happened he suggested that I follow these feelings and then he adjusted my medication.

I continued to work for John Tsamadas until about the end of January 1998. During that time I learned that he was not an honest man and that he truly didn't know what he was doing as far as paralegal work was concerned even though he had worked as one for over 20 years. I stopped working for him because he never really paid me. This is when I started working as an agency nurse going to various hospitals.

While I was working as a paralegal assistant I tried to stay in touch with Susan. I even wanted to have custody and visitation rights with Joshua. I also stayed in touch with Lynn a lady I had worked with in the past.

Susan moved out of the town home and in with the guy she had been having the affair with. This is when John had me convince him to use the town home since it was vacant. When this happened he set up visitation rights for me.

John was very two faced because he had been in contact with Susan during this divorce process. He even ended up having both of us in his office. Eventually he was able to have both of us agree to the final divorce agreement. The only part left was the waiting.

Around the end of February of 1998 my psychiatrist passed away. He died of cancer. This meant that I had to find a new one that would supply me with medication.

I continued attending my military drills in February. I mainly did so because it was a way to continue to get some money coming in since I still did not have a steady income. I also knew that this drill would be one of the last ones I would attend for a while.

While at this drill I had a problem concentrating. Part of the reason is because I was coming completely off of my psychiatric medication.

Another reason I was under stress again, mainly due to being financially unstable. I did make it through the weekend though.

By the end of February 1998 I was able to finally land another full time job. The new position was with Anaheim General Hospital. It was a charge nurse position on the 3-11 shift and I was to start the first part of March.

As I had mentioned I stayed in touch with my friend Lynn. In my eyes I considered our relationship one of dating but in reality it was one of being just friends. I helped her by working on her computer because working on computers had become a hobby of mine now. I also helped her out financially by lending her $400.00.

I continued to have my feelings of major depression. As I dwelled on those almost 11 years of marriage and the hurt that Susan and I suffered during those years, I realized that all of it could have been avoided had we both talked with and truly worked together at our marriage. The bad and most hurting part of all is that Joshua had to be a part of all of this.

Lynn was very supportive in my life. She would give me a woman's prospective of everything that has been going on. She was a true friend. This is why I chose to help her out financially.

The new job was not going very well. I was very stressed out mainly because I was not handling the position well. I was expected to know everything and truly was not catching on as well as I should have because I was emotionally unstable and distracted. This was seen by me yelling at my peers, making medication errors, and how I responded to an emergency situation where a patient died.

On April 7, 1998 I was called into my boss's office. At I thought that he was going to promote me as we talked about. What ended up happening is he was giving me a warning and was going to fire me soon. This all upset me so much that I faked being sick and left my shift early never to return at this hospital again. I know that I made this rash decision because I have been completely off of my medication.

Shortly after this happened I allowed John to take advantage of me again. He had me get a signature loan for another $10,000.00 for him. He also had me sign up for various credit cards and another car for the new attorney he was working with.

I turned in the T-Bird automobile back to the dealer after I knew that the motor, transmission, and brakes were going out on it. Since I no longer had a job I decided to make another decision.

Transitioning Male-to Female
April 7, 1998.

My cross-dressing took on a new level. I decided to see how well I could do being dressed in female clothing in public. This is when I went to TJ-MAX to shop.

I did my shopping in a mini-skirt, hose, heels, and no wig. I then went to the bank and closed the Roth account I started for my self several months before. Later that day I purchased a long hair auburn wig, some more shoes, a blouse, and a jacket.

After I ate I decided to check out one of the local nightclubs. While there I decided to drink. Due to my emotional state and paranoia, I got drunk very quickly. This is when I called Lynn and told her what was going on. She stayed with me on the cell phone until I made it home safely.

Shortly after this incident I had one last visit with Joshua. We went to have our pictures taken at Glamour Shots. The visit was a fun one and I basically spoiled Joshua rotten by getting him anything he wanted.

The day after these pictures I met up with Lynn first for lunch and then at Glamour shots. We talked about what I was going through and the confusion I was experiencing. She was a good listener and thought that I looked pretty cute as a female. She also helped me to choose the name that I was going to start using. I then had my pictures taken as the new me. When I looked at them I finally decided 100% that I was going to continue to live this way. Later that month my divorce was finalized.

In May I tried to obtain a position as a secretary with a temporary agency. This involved taking various tests in word processing and Microsoft Office. I did well with using Microsoft Word, but when it came to the other programs I barely pasted the tests. I never did get hired on.

This is when I started to go to a gay bar called the Tin Lizzy Saloon. While there I met Allen the owner. Allen reminded me of an old movie character. He was always a sweetheart to everybody. If he could help someone out he would.

I hung around the bar as much as I could. I even started to play pool again and became pretty good at it. Allen even put me to work when he saw that I was desolate.

Again I hooked up with John. He was shocked when he saw how much I had changed. He did try to remain my friend though and offered me a position of being an associate paralegal. I informed him that I would think about it. He then rebuilt a home personal computer for me.

By May 19, 1998 I was very stressed out. The reason is because this was my son Joshua's 9th birthday. I did gather some money for him but I did something out of the ordinary even for me. I went to the house he was staying at which is where Susan lived as Paulajean (PJ for short). I arrived there early in the evening. I had 2 people I was going to help out with me at the time.

I still was in tears when Susan and Joshua came to my car a 1973 Mercedes Benz sedan. When they arrived Susan did not recognize me. After a few minutes when she did realize who I was she grabbed Joshua and the $50.00 I gave him for his birthday and headed back into her house.

The next day Susan contacted me and informed me that she wanted certain items from our divorce. I met with her but informed her that she had to hurry because I was headed out to dinner and then out supposedly on a date.

When we met she was very strait forward, cold, and still emotionless toward me. I made her get the items herself because I was still upset at her. I also was enjoying being in control in my new miniskirt.

We did start to talk, but it ended up becoming more than talking. It became a full-blown argument. It was like we were 2 women having a cat fight. She then left with Ian her boyfriend. I headed out.

Eventually I sought out psychiatric help again. I mainly did this because I thought that I was going completely crazy. I also continued to be used by John. I ended up at the Gay and Lesbian Center located in Garden Grove, California. Through them I started to see a therapist from Chapman University located in Orange, California.

I would see a therapist at least twice a week at first and then once a week. The therapy was for those that could not afford regular therapy. The cost was low because the therapists were students working toward their psychology degree.

I was invited by Allen to help out with the; "Gay Pride Parade" located in Long Beach, California. I was going to help by representing the Tin Lizzy Saloon. This involved decorating a van and walking the distance.

The day before I went to this parade I completely built a web site with pictures and parts of my transitioning story. I spent 24 hours straight doing so. I then headed over to Allen's bar and stayed there until it closed. When the bar closed we headed to his place and I spent the night.

The next morning we got up early. We loaded up the van and headed to Longbeach. Once there we parked the van and the headed out for breakfast which Allen paid for. After breakfast the parade got on the way. We spent about an hour decorating the van. It was getting windy so Allen let me use one of the jackets with the; "Tin Lizzy" Logo on it. Finally the parade started. Allen and I walked it and boy did we get the cheers.

Some of the folks saw my new web site and cheered me on even more. I ended up walking the distance with encouragement because I was doing this walk my first time in heels. Walking the route of the parade was a blast. For me this was my; "Coming out" party.

After the parade was over we headed back to the van. Earl drove us back to the Tin Lizzy Saloon. We unloaded the van and the partied into the evening. This time when the bar closed I headed home.

The funny thing I was pulled over by the police when I left the bar. They thought that I was drunk, but I wasn't. In fact, I had not been drinking at all. The embaracing part of being pulled over is that I was completely in transition and I had not had my name and identification changed yet. I was put through the typical sobriety tests and of course passed with flying colors even in my heels.

For the next couple of months after the parade I hung around the Tin Lizzy quite often. I also would go on line to chat rooms and X-rated dating sites. I even went out on some dates and had a great time.

Shortly after Fathers Day I decided to take Allen up on his invite to the Gay Pride parade in San Francisco, California. I figured that I would go but not do the walk this time. I did this because I felt than Allen had used me. I also went on an Aids walk with Allen because those that promised to go with him canceled out on him at the last minute.

By August 1998 I was able to see Joshua one last time. I met him after I had just had a weave done to my hair with extensions. I also started working as a Triage Nurse for a Hospice Home Health agency.

The visit with Josh went well, but the job didn't. I say this because I was more interested in having fun on a date than going to see a patient who ended up going to the hospital. There also were other incidents, which I was involved in that cost me loosing this job.

During the month of September I was out of work again. I did manage to land a position doing private duty, but the bulk of the position was not going to start until October 1998. I also had already started the procedure for getting my name changed legally. John helped me with this by helping me get the paperwork put together.

At the end of September I ended up in the Psychiatric Crisis Center and I was placed on a 72-hour observation hold. While in the hospital this time I learned who my friends really were. My parents didn't even want to have anything to do with me. Neither did John.

Shortly after being released from the hospital I was still very brittle. I contacted John and he helped me to get my car fixed. Of course this was not free either.

I did start a 1-to-1 private duty case in Irvine, California on the night shift. The Mercedes was not reliable so I traded it in for a 1994 Chevrolet Blazer. I was also on the psychotropic medication Paxil by this time.

Working the night shift was very hard for me. I had days when I had a problem with staying awake. Eventually this case was given to Maxim Home Care and I moved with the case, but I was not receiving the pay that regular RN's received. After working the case for about 3 months I was able to move to the day shift.

While on the day shift I was able to meet the patient's family. His name was Frank and he had been completely dependant on nursing for all of his care. His mom and dad were into computers so because of my hobby I fit right in.

When I had worked with Frank about 6 months I started to case manage his case. I did this because no one else from the Maxim agency would do so. I also started to take Frank on outings, which he enjoyed.

I allowed him to have some kind of quality of life even though he was ventilator and wheelchair dependent.

In August 1999 Frank wanted to go to Las Vegas, Nevada for his birthday. Maxim would not allow the trip so I chose to sell myself as a private nurse for the trip.

We did make the trip and Frank had a great time. I helped him gamble and he did come back ahead by about $60.00. His sister and cousin made out a lot better.

Toward the end of the trip I did not get much sleep. Frank had a rough night and had to be suctioned quite often. I also made sure that he received his tube feeding without aspirating.

On the way home I was afraid. The reason is because Frank's ventilator started to alarm. This meant that it was on battery mode, which would only last for a short time. In fact, Frank's family laughed at me because they knew we would get Frank home without any problems.

When I was finishing with working with Frank's bed bath on September 13, 1999 I got hurt. This happened when I was placing him on a Hoyer lift sling. His weight and my weight caused me to twist my left thumb back. Being a critical care nurse I was able to pop it back into place but it still didn't feel right.

I completed the transfer to his wheelchair and then took some Motrin. We then talked about what happened. I was able to complete my shift and headed home.

The next day we went through the same routine, but shortly after I transferred Frank to his wheelchair my left hand froze up. I called Maxim and they could not get me any relief so they had me complete my shift and then come to the office. I then was sent to the clinic and had x-rays and tests done on my hand.

I was not able to work so Maxim assigned another person to care for Frank. I was placed on complete short-term disability and had to report for rehabilitation.

For me the rehabilitation did not go well. I could barely use my left hand. To add to this I had to transport myself to and from my appointments while driving my standard shift Blazer. Just driving was very painful but I was able to make it to these appointments.

In October 1999 I had Cortisone short to my left wrist. Getting the shot was very painful and the doctor giving me the shot did not listen to me. He just kept poking the syringe into my left wrist.

About a week after getting this shot I had an orthopedic doctor consult. The doctor placed my left arm into a cast. By having my arm this way I was not able to do too much. I even had a hard time driving my Blazer, but I still had to make my appointments.

Having my arm in a cast was a terrible experience. It started to itch and I had a problem with simple things like getting dressed. I also was very depressed about the whole thing. I was able to play pool though and with the cast I became pretty good at it. I even came in second place at the Tin Lizzy Saloon when they had a tournament.

Being a nurse I chose to cut the cast off by myself about a week earlier than it was going to be taken off in the first place. I was not happy with the care I was getting so I had John find me an attorney that would get me another doctor and my lawsuit on the road. That happened about a week or so later.

I was contacted for a deposition from Maxim's attorney. For this deposition I had to drive to Las Angeles, California which was about 45 miles from my apartment.

During the deposition they felt that my transitioning might have caused the injury. I assured them that I am a good nurse and that the injury to my arm was a fluke or freak accident.

After the deposition I contacted my attorney and told him what I had said. He worked with me to get a psychological and physical evaluation on my left hand and arm. I also continued with my therapy, this time with a new psychologist I had met through the Gay and Lesbian Center. Now I was seeing a psychiatrist and psychologist at the same time. I even was tested to see where I stood psychologically.

The new surgeon determined that I needed to have carpal tunnel surgery with a thumb release. He also found out that I had Reflex Sympathetic Dystrophy Syndrome (RFDS). The most severe part was on my left arm but I actually had this disease on both arms. He treated me symptomatically and had me scheduled for surgery by February 2000.

While I was awaiting my surgery I decided to try to clean up the debt that John and I accrued through the credit cards and that signature loan. John helped me gather everything together and create the documents for filing a bankruptcy. We found in the process that there was a judgment against me on the vehicle I turned in. I did file the bankruptcy paperwork by November 1999.

During all of this time I had been tried on different medications. I was even given Depokote with my Paxil, which made me violently sick. On my birthday I decided to have a good meal, and just pamper myself. This was hard to do because I had been up all night getting sick from the Depokote.

In January 2000 I continued to go to therapy at least once a week. We also prepared for my surgery in February. I never was sure when everything was going to happen, so I kept bugging my doctor.

The surgery went well in February. I had minimal swelling and less pain than before the surgery. I had to follow-up with therapy 3 days after the surgery and the for about another 8 weeks.

Around this time I tried to help out others less fortunate than me. First I helped 2 drug addicts, and they ended up destroying my furniture. This happened because they were actually both hooked on Heroin.

Next I had a male move in with me. He belittled and embarrassed me quite a few times and I eventually had dropped him off in Anaheim, California. After I dropped him off he was arrested and tried to hook up with me again.

I also tried to help out 2 lesbian girls. To me this was a disaster because all they wanted to do was get high on booze and marijuana. The reason I say it was a disaster is because I too partied with them.

Next I hooked up with a lady named Joanna. She was very depressed and was about to loose her apartment. I helped her out by putting her stuff into storage and moving her in with me. This didn't work out because Joanna kept getting into my makeup and personal things.

Shortly after I had the surgery to my left had my disability dropped drastically. This is when I tried to have 2 other transsexuals move in with me. I did all of the cooking and they did not want to help me by helping me keep the apartment clean. We all were always fighting, which made it harder for me to concentrate.

Since I had so much time off I decided to write my family and let them know what I was doing. I apologized to my mom for not being honest with her all of these years and for using some of her clothing to cross-dress in the past. I also wrote my sister and told her the same thing.

I completed my rehabilitation by June 2000. This is when I started to job hunt again. I had a hard time finding work due to my disability and previous job history. I even worked with the rehabilitation agency for several months to get me working again. The agency even sent me to a seminar to obtain a Case Management Certification.

In late November 2000 I went to an open house at Kindred Healthcare. During this open house I was hired immediately as a charge nurse. By December 2000 I was working again and doing a good job.

In January 2001 I also landed a position as a Clinical Instructor for LVN's with Concord Career Institute. I was going to start during the spring session and work part time 2 days a week on the 3-11 shift. Again I did well with this position. I continued to work both of these positions until the summer.

While working at Kindred I became pretty good at my position. I learned that I could manage the shift with the least amount of stress and conflict. I also saw that I was being taken advantage of due to being in transition. I also saw this when one of the female respiratory therapists accused me of sexual harassment when I felt had done nothing to provoke her.

By the end of 2000 I finally received the payoff on my lawsuit with Maxim Health Care. I saved the money and planned a trip for my reassignment surgery for late July 2001. I was able to save quite a bit by that time.

The New Me, a Surgically Created Female
July 2001

Finally July 2001 came and I was headed for Bangkok, Thailand for my Sexual Reassignment Surgery (SRS). I had one of my transsexual roommates take me to Los Angeles International Airport. The trip on the airplane took about 16 hours even with the 2 stops that we made.

Once I arrived at Bangkok everything went very quickly. I received about 5 hours sleep and headed to see my surgeon. By about 3:30pm I was headed to the hospital. Shortly after we arrived at the hospital I was rushed to my room and prepped for Surgery.

At around 5:30pm I was given a Halcion sleeping pill and was wheeled into the surgical suite. The next thing I remember is I was back in my room by about 7:30pm. The SRS surgery took only 1-½ hours. Toward the end of the surgery I started to wake up but I was put back under at my request.

The next day the nurses tried to assist with getting me out of bed. I could not get up even with their help, but by that evening I was able to get up on my own. I ended up with the binding of my breasts and the packing of my newly formed vaginal area for 5 days.

Once everything was removed I was able to examine myself for the first time. This is when I became very happy and thought that my surgeon did an awesome job with my surgery. I still was having pain, but I was able to work through this on my own. I also had a problem with urinary incontinence due to having a Foley catheter for the last 5-6 days. I knew in time that once I healed more I would regain control of these new body parts. I was released from the hospital after the 6th day in the hospital.

The nurse that met with me at the Bangkok airport came to see me in my room. He taught me how to care for myself including self-dilatation.

111

It took me some time to learn all of this but after some practice I was able to learn what to do.

On day seven we had planned an outing. This gave me the opportunity to do some shopping in Bangkok and try out the new me in public. We even were able to do some sight seeing in the process which I enjoyed. A couple days later I was going to be headed back to the United States.

The day before I left the surgeon examined me. He informed me that everything he did with the surgery looked fine. He also reinforced that I continue to clean my new vaginal area and do my dilatation at least once a day. I also informed him that there were a couple of sutures irritating me, but he informed me everything was normal. The next day I was headed back home.

I arrived at Los Angeles International airport (LAX) 16-to-20 hours later. My transsexual friend Susan met me at LAX. She made sure that we got home safely. A couple of days later I returned back to work even though I was pretty sore when I sat down. I was able to manage with the help of using a rubber doughnut when I sat down.

On September 11, 2001 while I was at work I saw the twin towers destroyed. At first when I saw the incident on television in a patient's room I thought to myself that it looked like a great movie. Then as I listened further I realized that the towers were destroyed. This is when I befriended one of our patients. Her name was Jacquelyn Ramsey. She was in the hospital because she had congestive heart failure and required wound care.

When I was at work I would share bible verses with her. She appreciated this and these verses actually helped her to get better. I also would spend some time talking and praying with her.

By the end of spring 2002 I lost my teaching position. This happened because the students did not appreciate the evaluations that I gave them. They also decided that they didn't like a transgendered instructor that was giving them a break.

Hoag hospital also did not care for the way I was teaching the students. I knew that part of this was because Susan was working on staff there now. When this happened I decided that would try to get back into the military.

In early July 2002 I went back east to visit my brother Ron and his family. We actually saw the sight where the twin towers were destroyed on September 11, 2001. Besides seeing this sight we also were able to visit the Fireman's memorial, and George Washington's home at Mount Vernon. It actually was a very good visit.

By September 2002 I was assigned to Brook Army Medical Center (BAMC) for my first assignment as a female officer with the United States Army. I was able to relearn how to function in the Surgical ICU. It was only for 2 weeks but for me the training was a good experience. I did well during this training.

While assigned at BAMC I remained in contact with Jacque. We talked with each other many times when I got off of work. I also remained in contact with one of the ministers of the church I belonged too. I made it home after I completed my 2 weeks.

Prior to going one for this training one of my best friends died of cancer. This friend accepted me as family when I started my transitioning and remained a friend until the end. Jacque was even able to meet this person and was there for me when she saw that I could not handle it when a loved friend died.

By January 2003 I received orders to return to BAMC for an activation or deployment due to the Iraqi war. I was to report to BAMC by March 19, 2003. What this meant is that I had to put my belongings into storage. I also was going to leave my new best friend behind. I remember even breaking into tears telling Jacque that it was hard for me to live my life this way.

The day before I left Jacque and my new friends threw a goodbye party for me. This is when I discovered that others cared about me leaving. It was an enjoyable time. I left by 3:00pm the next day in my new 2001 PT Cruiser packed to the brim with clothes and items I had forgotten to pack.

I made the trip to San Antonio, Texas in 2 ½ days. The reason it took this long was because I chose not to drive during the night. I also chose to drive only 8-to-12 hours at a time. I made it to San Antonio, Texas about a day early.

A New Life in San Antonio, Texas

Once I arrived in San Antonio I tried to report in early. I was told that I would have to wait until the next day. When I was told this, I was also told that I would be reimbursed for staying in a motel and for my trip to Texas since I drove the whole trip. Shortly after receiving this information I headed to a Drury motel near the I35 freeway and Walzem boulevard and ended up staying the night. I also had a meal at a Jim's restaurant near the motel. I remember even locking myself out of my room a couple of times before finally getting settled in for the night.

On March 19, 2003 I checked in to the Battalion as I was supposed to do. While doing so I met with the other nurses and we received a brief orientation. After the orientation we were assigned rooms at the local Guest House. I wasn't sure that I was going to stay in the room so I checked out a Select Hilton located on the other side of the base.

Once I saw the small room at the Hilton, I decided that the Guest House would be the best place to stay for the money. This is when I made sure that I had a room on the lower floor because of my disability. After we decided on the room, I completely unpacked my PT Cruiser. I spent part of the night setting up my new room since it was going to be home for a while.

Orientation to BAMC took about 2 weeks. Immediately after the orientation I was assigned to the Surgical ICU that I had worked at about 6 months prior. I found out that I was going to be the Officer in Charge (OIC) or Head Nurse of this unit which to me was .an unexpected surprise.

I tried to run this in a very strict manner unit right off of the bat. This was hard to do because I received resistance right from most of the staff from the beginning. This is why I decided to enroll in the accelerated charge nurse course that was taking place the first week there actually on the same floor that the SICU was located. After I completed the course I got involved with the staffing and scheduling. I even had staff meetings.

About 2 months after running the unit I was replaced by a regular army Major. The main reason I was reassigned was because the nurses thought that I was too tough on them. They also knew that I would fill in during the night shift when they were missing a nurse. Having already worked 8 hours they knew that this was not safe for the patient. This is when I was assigned to the Special Procedures section of the hospital.

When I was transferred to this new unit I broke down into tears. I thought that I truly messed up while being in charge of the SICU. The other reason for the tears was because I had injured my left shoulder during a physical training test earlier during that day. I did agree with my immediate supervisor to try this new position on a temporary basis.

At first it seemed like I was catching on to this new position slowly. I then panicked when I over sedated one of the patients during a procedure. After this happened one of the nurses accused me of attacking her. She stated I choked her when I never touched her. When this happened I was removed from BAMC by the military police (MP's) and taken off to the military jail. Shortly after being taken to jail, I started to have another nervous breakdown. This happened mainly because I knew I never touched the individual and no one believed me. I felt that I was being signaled out because I was different being a transsexual in the military.

I was bailed out by my commanding officer but I was still in tears when this happened. I informed her that I was accused unjustly. She didn't want to hear it and wrote me up for no reason. She then recommended that the psychological department see me.

I listened to her and informed the sociologist and psychiatrist that I would be better if I was out of the military especially when I was falsely accused of something that never happened. I visited this psychology department at least once a week until my deployment was completed.

I was then transferred to the Medical ICU and tried to work there the best I can. The thing is my heart was not in it so I did as little as possible. I also was so doped up by the psychiatrist that I could barely function.

While living in the Guest House I talked with a lot of the peers about my age who have just returned from Iraq. I listened to a lot of terrible stories about how dirty the . I also saw that the Reservist were not being taken care of as the regular army troops were.

In June 2003 I decided to see if I could purchase a house here in Texas. If I could I decided I would stay in Texas and start over. By mid-July everything was in place for me to purchase a home. I signed my final papers by the end of July and moved in by August 11th after I was released from my deployment. 5 days later I had my furniture delivered from California.

Around the time that all of this was happening my daughter finally contacted me. She informed me that she was in trouble for signing her husband's check and that he was going to have her put in jail for fraud. I talked with her and sent the money to bail her out directly to her bank. I did this because I still did not trust my her.

When I got out of the army I was all doped up on pain medication and psychotropic medication. I was on Neurontin, Paxil, Vicodin, and another medication that really messed me up.

Prior to coming to Texas I was not on any medication. I decided to come off of everything especially since I was allergic to most of them. The process took me about a month and I was lucky because I had minimal withdrawal symptoms this time.

On September 1, 2003 I decided to have an open house or house-warming party for myself. I invited a lot of people but no one showed up. I even cooked and everything. With this happening I again was depressed. I also realized that those that I met at BAMC that called me a friend were not true friends at all.

By mid-September my transfer from Kindred in California to Kindred San Antonio was finalized. The orientation to this new facility only took a couple of weeks. I was on the job for about 1-½ months when I had to have a cystoscopy. The reason for the cystoscopy was because I had so many urinary tract infections during 2003. After the procedure I returned back to work but again for me the job was not going well.

Loss of a Dear Friend

Jacque joined me here in Texas toward the end of October. When she got off of the train she looked terrible. Her skin was all gray and she had a problem with her breathing. Then Jacque got sick and never informed me about it.

When I was released from the hospital I checked in on her. She responded to me verbally so I thought nothing of it. Later I was called from BAMC and was told that I was to get my release paperwork before going back to work that evening. As I left I checked on Jacque again and she responded to me again with a, "Yeh, yeh, and a moan.".

After I left BAMC I headed to Denny's restaurant to eat before going to work. This is when I tried to call Jacque and I did not get a response. I tried to call again after I ate and still no response. I tried 2 other times and then I contacted a friend. I had them check on her.

When he couldn't get into the house he called the police at my request. About 30 minutes later I received a call that Jacque had died in her sleep. I was told that I had to identify the remains and try to assist or an investigation for wrongdoing would be done. I informed my supervisor about what happened and he allowed me to take care of this problem.

Once I arrive near my house I saw a bunch of police, a fire truck, and ambulance in front of my house. As they met me when I got out of my car, I was informed that Jacque had died. They informed me that they worked on her for about 50 minutes without success. I then was escorted to her room and I identified her. I was then asked if I knew anything about her and what was in her belongings. I informed them that I didn't know very much but that I would do what I could to find out. I did find a file that contained Jacque's dad's information. Shortly after finding this out I called a friend from church and informed her what had happened. This friend was Anita and she came right over.

New Friends and a New Family

Anita stayed with me until Jacque's remains were removed from the house. She and I talked during most of the time. We also prayed together and did some minor cleaning. Anita stayed with me until about 3:00am in the morning.

Later in the day I contacted some of Jacque's old friends. I basically told them how Jacque had died in her sleep. I also called Jacque's dad and gave him the details. He asked if Jacque was a Christian and I assured him she was. He informed me that Jacque had called him the day before and told him she was very sick. I then heard the story that her dad expected her to die before he did.

Later during this week Anita, her husband Richard, and Jean came over to visit with me. They assisted me with clearing out some of Jacque's things. They also prayed with me and gave me moral support.

I could not go into the room that Jacque died in for almost 3 months. This was even after her bed and everything had been already removed. I would have to keep the door closed due to the eerie feeling that I would get when I even passed the room.

When I did finally get past these eerie feelings, I decided to make this room an office, computer, and junk room instead of a bedroom again. That is when I moved all of my computer stuff heavy wooden desk into the room. I also had to clean up the blood and mess from the resuscitation attempt back in October.

By about April 2004 I had to have surgery for a spontaneous cyst/fistula. I had the surgery and ended being out of work for a couple of weeks. Shortly after the procedure is when I was taken advantage of again.

Speed (Eric Senior) convinced me to take him to Ohio. I found out after we arrived in Ohio that he had us transport drugs mainly marijuana. When I found this out I was pissed and I was ready to kill him by shooting him with my gun. Instead of wasting the trip I called my daughter. She agreed to let me see my grand-kids for the first time.

The drive to Pennsylvania took me about 6 hours. By the time I arrived at my daughter's home I was exhausted. As soon as I got there Tammy had already arranged for a sitter for her kids. We then headed for a local restaurant where I had dinner. While there we tried to become more acquainted. The next day I did enjoy wrestling with my grand-kids.

When I returned from my trip I was off of work for a few more days. Then I saw my doctor and received a release to return back to work. Shortly after returning back to work I continued to have problems at Kindred. These problems caused me so much stress that I voluntarily left my position. This is when I decided to try to work Home Health again.

The first position I held was as a Case Manager with Tricare Home Health. It was a fairly easy position compared to the positions I held in California. I stayed with them for about 3-to-4 months. I mainly left because there were no benefits.

The next place I worked was Pure Care. I was to work as the Associate Director of Nursing. I worked there only 1 month. The reason was because the records of the company were in a shambles. This agency also was very close to being closed down.

Finally I moved over to Home Health Innovations. The position I was to hold is that of Director of Quality Assurance. The thing is this was only a title because the owner had been paying a private agency to actually do their Quality Assurance.

I did try to do the best I could with this position. When I did audit charts and found problems, I was slapped on the wrist for being too tough. During the course of my position I also was assigned to be a triage nurse which was the type of position I did in California that caused me problems at another agency in the past.

While I was working these positions I tried to help out several street people again. The female only lasted 1 day. The next a male I tried to help, was very lazy. All he wanted to do was sleep, play on his computer, and drink beer. I did everything I could to help him out including letting him use one of my vehicles. He stayed with me for almost 4 months. Finally I had another male move in.

Initially everything appeared great with this new renter. He paid his rent on time, worked every day, and paid his child support. As I got to know him better I found that he was a felon that truly wanted to rehabilitate. This is why I had chosen to help him out.

For the first few months this individual was good about paying his rent. By the summer he tried to get out of doing so because he had very little money to live on. In fact, around this time he decided to steal from me and pawn items just to get by. Of course this was taking advantage of his living arrangements.

I eventually left Home Health Innovations by April 2005, mainly because I felt that I didn't fit in since I was the only white person working for the agency. I also felt that I was not appreciated and finally my temper got the best of me.

When I left, I was without a job. That is when I placed a copy of my resume on-line. Within 4 hours after placing my resume I was contacted by Nightingale Nurses (a nurse travel agency). They set me up with a contract working for the Baptist Health System here in San Antonio. I ended up working for them for over 6 months. Then I tried working with InteliStaf another temporary nursing agency,

I stayed active with InteliStaf for about 6 months. The reason I didn't continue working with them is because they could not get me enough work. This is why I applied with the Baptist Health System. I was able to land a position Southeast Baptist Hospital by November 2005.

I worked at Southeast Baptist Hospital in the ICU. I stayed with them for over 6 months. Then I started to have problems with my peers. They would no longer help me and it was upsetting me. I would demonstrate what I was feeling by making harmless nonsensical comments.

When this happened they decided to make an example of me and forced me to voluntarily terminate my position. I then tried to work as a Director of Nursing at a Skilled Nursing Facility located in Pearsall, Texas. This position only lasted 5 days. The reason that it only lasted this long is because the staff did not like me and the administrator did not want to take the time to train me.

In April 2006 I hooked up with Texas Work-Source again. Through them I was able to apply for various nursing positions. By mid-April I landed an interview with the San Antonio State Hospital. I was hired and actually started work May 1, 2006. The position I was hired for was that of a Float Nurse in the 11-7 shift. This is the position that I continue to hold today.

Today, Some Stability in My Life

As I am completing my ninth year since transitioning from Male-to-Female, and my first year working for the State of Texas, I have discovered that I have found an area that I have never thought I would be good at. This is the area of Psychiatric Nursing. Here are some insights.

Throughout my 20 plus years being involved in the medial field I have seen and worked with patients with many medical, social, and psychological problems. I believe that the reason I am good in psyche is because I have experienced and dealt with my own problems as a patient myself for over 30 years. In a sense, "I have been on the other side of the fence." Yes, this means that I had been a patient at one time or another.

The other thing I have learned through experience is to listen and treat the person as a whole individual and not the disease process. To empathize and not sympathize with the patients I care for. Now you might ask is this an easy thing to do? Does it work? How does it affect you? Here are some answers I have found.

For me, since I am a people person, I try to interact with the patients face to face. The problem though is I have issues of my own when dealing with anxiety. While working with others I try to have the individual respond to me. If this means I have to walk with the patient or get closer I do. I also use the knowledge I have learned throughout my years in nursing to keep me in perspective on ways to treat those with a mental illness handicap. By doing all of these things I find that I learn more about with is going on with the patients I care for.

I have found for me when I treat a patient, as I would like to be treated I find that my success rate has been pretty good. Most patients I deal with try to respect me. At times some of them consider me their favorite nurse.

I believe that by working as a psychiatric nurse that I can help those less fortunate than me. For me this is very rewarding and why I became a nurse in the first place.

We all have our highs and lows, our depression and mania. It is how each of us responds to these feelings. Each of us will always respond differently. Sometimes we respond in a positive manner and other times in a destructive and negative manner.

Over the past 25 years I have seen a tremendous amount of growth as a nurse and as an individual. I have learned that the problems I have are very mild compared to the problem I see others deal with each and every day when I am at work. I also have seen the same thing when I am not working. This is why I feel that I have been and am blessed to just be alive and able to work.

Summary, Life is Good.

As you can see from this autobiography a lot has happened in my life of 50 plus years in this world. To date my immediate family still remains very dysfunctional and distant in my life. They continue to have a problem with accepting things that are new and different from the way that they were brought up. An example of this are the changes I have made in my life including my transitioning.

My dad continues to argue and be abusive toward my mom. He remained this way until he died in August of 2009. I went to the wake in Milwaukee, Wisconsin, but could not handle dealing with all of the family issues and lies.

Mom continued to take the abuse because she feels that she can't live without my dad. Even though she complained about the abuse but when someone tries to step in and help her she refuses the assistance and denies that there is a problem.

You will see that through each of the marriages that I had been through there never was complete stability. The problem is I had a big problem being completely honest with who I was and about my cross-dressing and being a latent transsexual. In hindsight I see that this was wrong, but I also believe that even if I had been honest the circumstances would not have been any different.

Not everyone has had the opportunity to experience traveling as a hitchhiker. For me this experience has taught me that in the 1970's people would help hikers get around. Yes, doing so was dangerous back then and it continues to be a bad way to travel or get around the country even today.

Being poor and living in the streets as a street person is no fun. I saw this during my trip to Canada, and when I first lived in California. These experiences are the main reason I push myself to continue to work even when I don't want too. I do not want to be poor or live in the streets again especially today with all of the hate crimes toward those of us who are different.

I do not believe that everyone who is truly transsexual should have to go through a lot of the torment, hate, or verbal attacks that I have had to experience when I went through my changes. In some ways I was treated worse than a human being or even an animal. This happened because of ignorance, bias opinions, and at times per se' "Christian beliefs." We are all God's children no matter what. I feel that we should be treated the way that we want to be treated.

Many of us when we cross-dress whether we are male or female do so for other reasons besides sexual arousal. Sometimes we do this just to be comfortable. Of course there are those who dress this way for the arousal. That is why there is always; "Two sides to the coin."

Then there are those as myself who have been suffering from gender dysphoria or gender identity confusion disorder. We dress opposite the gender we have been born into because our minds and bodies don't match who we are. This is usually how one knows that they are a transsexual.

When deciding to make any changes in your life, my suggestion is to be sure and true to yourself. Make sure that if you decide to change your gender by having surgery that you have really received a lot of psychological therapy first. Then make sure that when you have had the surgery that you can live with these new changes no matter what happens to you. I say this because there are many male-to-female and female-to-male transsexuals that have committed suicide within the first 10 years after transitioning.

I believe that the reason this happens is because they had come to a conclusion that they had made a mistake and can't live with who they are. Remember this is your life and you need to truly be happy with yourself. It also is no about the fantasy of being the other sex. It is about reality. As long as you stay in reality, you should be able to live as you please.

Finally as I stated I have been blessed. I say this because early in my life I chose to become a nurse. Being a nurse has helped me understand who I am today. Even though I receive medication today, I use what I have learned to help others. I even went a step further and became a registered nurse with a Bachelors of Science Degree in Nursing and a Master's Degree in Healthcare Administration. I hope that you enjoyed what you have read.

About the Author

P.J. Anderson is an individual who has experienced a lot of situations during her lifetime. She definitely has learned and grown through these. This book is the third of three that she has written. The first was an autobiography called: "THREE STRIKES AND YOU ARE NOT OUT," and a series here, "A WORLD OF ABUSE," "I CRY FROM WITHIN," "STAGES," and "ALL OF MY CHILDREN."

She has developed a Web site that she started 11 years ago in California. It is: http://www.geocities.com/pj_1953/page2 that has been discontinued because the Geocities.com main web site no longer exists. She first started her writing career at the age 11 years old. She has received awards and went summer to camp for her story "FATMAN and BOY BLUBBER." and presently publishes an annual news letter for her family and friends called; "THE TEXAS ALPHA." At one time Ms Anderson ran and published a newsletter for the nursing ministry at The First Church of Christ in Garden Grove, California.

Ms Anderson has been a registered nurse over 22 years and obtained a Masters degree in Healthcare Administration Nursing in 2009. She also has been working with computers since the late 1970's and holds an Associate's degree in this area.

From 2000-2002 Ms Anderson also ran two support groups with the Gay and Lesbian Center of Orange County California. One group was People Experiencing an Alternative Lifestyle (PEAL). The other was called the South Coast Transgender Alliance (SCTA). One group dealt with Transgender issues both male and female. The other dealt with drug and alcohol abuse at various levels.

Ms Anderson was born as in Milwaukee, Wisconsin and has been living as her true self (female) for the past 12 years. She now resides in the San Antonio, Texas area.